The

Software

Architect's

Profession

An Introduction

D1114153

ISBN 0-13-060796-7

90000

9 780130 607966

WWW.WWISA.ORG

The Worldwide Institute of Software Architects (WWISA)
is a non-profit professional organization dedicated to establishing
a formal profession of software architecture and providing information
and services to software architects and their clients—analogous to the formation
of the American Institute of Architects roughly 140 years ago. The essential tenet of WWISA is that
there is a perfect analogy between building and software architecture, and that the classical role of the
architect needs to be introduced into the software construction industry.

The architect, whether designing structures of brick or computer code, forms the bridge between the
world of the client and that of the technical builders. This critical bridge has been missing from the
software industry, resulting in a decades-long software crisis. Entire software structures are
dysfunctional or have been scrapped entirely—before seeing a single "inhabitant." We have simply been
building huge, complex structures without architects, and without blueprints.

WWISA was established in 1998 and now has over 1,500 members in over 50 countries. Membership is
open to practicing and aspiring software architects, professors, students, CIOs, and CEOs. Members
participate to promote training and degree programs, develop architectural standards and guiding
principles, and work toward creating a standard body of shared knowledge. We are our client
advocates; clients are our driving force. We hope to become the clients' bridge to successful software
construction by helping them leverage the full range of technology.

SERIES VISION

Software technology is critically important to the world's businesses and human society. However, software engineering remains a chaotic, immature discipline, unable to systematically deliver successful systems. What's missing is software architecture. But, many questions about software architecture, going much deeper than academic discussions, remain unresolved. In particular, how do we apply software architecture on real-world projects and across business enterprises?

At the same time, many successful practitioners of software architecture know how to answer these questions from experience. From among these practitioners our series authors are carefully selected. Often they work in companies that rely upon software system success as their core business model (e.g., business systems, telecommunications, and financial services). These innovative software architects have developed systematic disciplines for doing work that consistently surpasses the industry averages for on-time, on-budget deliveries that meet users' needs and expectations. Some of these experts utilize published standards and patterns for software architecture. Others can share unique lessons learned through professional experience. We have discovered significant commonalities in practical software architecture knowledge which can be useful across most software applications. Together, the joint knowledge of innovative software architects represents the next generation of practice for leading technologists in the software discipline.

The mission of the Software Architecture Series is to publish a common body of knowledge for the software architecture discipline. Software architecture is a specialty distinct from software engineering, programming, and project management. A software architect balances and resolves design forces from many perspectives, including system stakeholders and system developers. Software architects are responsible for a much wider and more interesting range of issues (technical, intuitive, and human factors) than we typically associate with project management. Software architects create technical plans that coordinate the work of groups of programmers, resolving significant systemwide risks and project/technical inefficiencies. The software architect role is an important career path for lead programmers and other IT professionals, as an alternative to project management.

In this series, our goal is to establish the knowledge base for the software architect career path. We hope to share the comprehensive knowledge of successful software architects in a way that fundamentally changes how people develop software, to show better ways of working, and to develop individuals (such as yourselves) into world-class professionals drawing from the acquired knowledge of a wide range of peers in the software architecture profession. We share these goals with a nonprofit organization, the Worldwide Institute of Software Architecture (WWISA), a co-sponsor of this book series.

In conclusion, knowledge is power, particularly for software architects. We are giving to you—the next generation of software architects—the best of our knowledge in the hope that you will fundamentally change the software profession, through your individual practices, toward a mature discipline, which achieves systematic success in the development of software systems. We hope that you as software architects derive all of the benefits and professional recognition that is due to you. In this transition, we do not expect your personal career to be trouble-free and easy. But we do know that software architecture is one of the most exciting fields of endeavor, and we welcome you into our worldwide community!

THOMAS J. MOWBRAY, PH.D.
SERIES EDITOR

Software Architecture Series

Thomas J. Mowbray, Ph.D., Series Editor

▶ *Confessions of a Software Architect*
Bowman

▶ *Software Architecture: Organizational Principles and Patterns*
Dikel, Kane, Wilson

▶ *Software Architect Bootcamp*
Malveau, Mowbray

▶ *Architecting with RM-ODP*
Putman

▶ *Design of Software Architecture*
Scheer

▶ *Software Architecture: An Introduction to the Profession*
Sewell, Sewell

The Software Architect's Profession

An Introduction

Marc T. Sewell
Laura M. Sewell

Prentice Hall PTR
Upper Saddle River, NJ 07458
www.phptr.com

Library of Congress Cataloging-in-Publication Data
Sewell, Marc T.,
   The software architect's profession: an introduction/Marc T. Sewell and Laura M. Sewell.
      p. cm.—(Software architecture series)
   Includes bibliographical references and index.
   ISBN 0-13-060796-7 (pbk)
     1. Computer software. 2. Computer architecture. I. Sewell, Laura M., II. Title. III. Series

   QA76.754 .S47 2001
   005.3—dc21

                                                                    2001036328

Editorial/Production Supervision: *Argosy*
Acquisitions Editor: *Paul Petralia*
Editorial Assistant: *Justin Somma*
Marketing Manager: *Debby Van Dijk*
Manufacturing Manager: *Alexis R. Heydt-Long*
Cover Design: *Nina Scuderi*
Cover Design Director: *Jerry Votta*
Art Director: *Gail Cocker-Bogusz*
Illustrations: *Marty J. Luko*
Interior Design: *Meg Van Arsdale*
Project Coordinator: *Anne R. Garcia*

© 2002 Prentice Hall PTR
Prentice-Hall, Inc.
Upper Saddle River, NJ 07458

The publisher offers discounts on this book when ordered in bulk quantities.
For more information, contact
Corporate Sales Department,
Prentice Hall PTR
One Lake Street
Upper Saddle River, NJ 07458
Phone: 800-382-3419; FAX: 201-236-7141
E-mail (Internet): corpsales@prenhall.com

10 9 8 7 6 5 4 3 2 1

ISBN 0-13-060796-7

Pearson Education LTD.
Pearson Education Australia PTY, Limited
Pearson Education Singapore, Pte. Ltd.
Pearson Education North Asia Ltd.
Pearson Education Canada, Ltd.
Pearson Educación de Mexico, S.A. de C.V.
Pearson Education—Japan
Pearson Education Malaysia, Pte. Ltd.
Pearson Education, Upper Saddle River, New Jersey

Contents

Contents
—

Foreword

Andrea Palladio is one of the most influential architects of all times. His seminal work—*The Four Books of Architecture*, published in Venice in 1570—had an immediate and profound influence upon Renaissance construction. Palladio's genius lay in his ability to distill the essence of Roman architectural principles, build upon them to establish a broad vocabulary for the entire domain of architecture, and then articulate a set of pragmatic rules to aid the architect in creating functional yet beautiful structures. As Palladio noted, "Three things...ought to be considered in every fabric, without which no edifice will deserve to be commended; and these are utility or convenience, strength, and beauty." Palladio was passionate about his profession, and through his writings was able to share that passion.

Marc and Laura are equally passionate about the emerging profession of the software architect. In this book, they share their deep experience in the pragmatics of that trade. With clear parallels to the history of architecture, from Imhotep to Le Corbusier, from I. M. Pei to Christopher Alexander, the authors offer a clear statement as to what the role of the software architect is, what it is not, and what it can be.

Software is the ultimate building material, infinitely malleable and incapable of wearing out. Economic forces lead us to build systems of increasing complexity and thus, because of our fundamental human limitations in coping with complexity, we abstract. The history of software engineering is, therefore, the history of abstraction. In the drive to higher levels of abstraction, functional decomposition was superseded by object-oriented design. Next, design patterns surfaced, giving the development team a vocabulary sufficient to talk about the mechanisms formed by societies of objects. Beyond design patterns lay architectural frameworks, representing common, significant design decisions that shape the structure and behavior of entire systems. Indeed, the presence (or absence) of a strong architectural vision is a key predictor in the success (or failure) of a complex system. As such, the importance of the role of the software architect has grown. This trade is in its fledgling state, but in this book, Marc and Laura establish it as a true profession, something that can be learned and that is worthy of pursuit in and of itself.

If you are already a software architect, this book will give you a broader perspective that will help you become more effective in your role. If you aspire to become a software architect, then this book will help you in your journey by explaining the meaning of architecture, the process of architectural design, and the pragmatics of the profession, from ethical considerations to deep technical activities.

As software professionals, we seek to build useful things that work, using a process that is both efficient and economical. The software architect has the demanding yet incredibly rewarding opportunity to lead the construction of such systems. Thus, at its best, just as Palladio notes, the software architect can craft beautiful systems.

May you also go on to build beautiful software.

Grady Booch
Chief Scientist
Rational Software Corporation

Preface

It's fun to be on the right side of a transformation. Being on the wrong side is frustrating, because nothing ever seems to fit. Some people make it through the change, others don't. To do so requires a shift in the way we see, an alteration of what psychologists call our *mental set*. That is the purpose of this book: To change the way people see software design and construction, supplying the reader with a new cognitive map.

This is not a technical book—on purpose. We present the case that there is a perfect analogy between constructing a building and constructing software and that this analogy is the tool for making the transformation. If we delved deeply into the familiar terms and practices of software design and construction, readers with technical backgrounds would be pulled down by the thick layer of associations and habits they have built up in their minds from experience—hindering change.

Instead, we talk largely about building architecture and construction, bringing the subject back to the software industry to illustrate the truisms of the analogy. We hope the reader is able to really see architecture and construction—the history, roles, and processes—from a fresh perspective, not in the light cast from their software experience. Seeing architecture and construction in their classical forms creates a separate template in the mind, one that can then be superimposed on the familiar milieu of software construction. In this way, the transformation can take place and we can build software predictably and reliably.

The analogy is the tool that makes things fit. Don't be fooled by its seeming simplicity. Simplicity does not equate with superficiality, and something does not have to be impossibly confusing to be profound. Buildings are highly complex and their construction difficult, but everyone understands how they get built and the roles of those involved. That clarity of role and process is what is missing from software construction. Bringing the clarity to the software industry is what the transformation is about.

This book is written for a broad audience of technical and nontechnical people alike. It can be understood by anyone and would be helpful to clients of software projects, software professionals, students, and interested inhabitants of software systems. Clients are especially important because they are driving this transformation—not academia or software professionals.

In the 1990s, clients and employers began to use an architectural approach to software construction. They bestowed the new title of *architect* on software professionals, wrote their job descriptions, and established architecture departments.

Even those clients and employers not in sync with the analogy saw a need for the architectural role. They created the title CTO and assigned this person the guardianship of the technology, enterprise architecture, and software strategy. They only erred with the title. This person is fulfilling the role of chief architect.

The clients have a natural, intuitive understanding of the analogy. It gives them a mental image needed to understand and manage software construction and, simply stated, it just seems right to them to design something first and then carefully build it under the supervision of the guardian of the design.

We hope this book will, in its small way, give the reader insights into architecture along with a tool for thinking in a new way.

Marc and Laura Sewell
marcandlaura@wwisa.org

architect / ˈɑːkɪtɛkt / *n. & v.* M16. [Fr. *architecte* f. It. *architetto,* or their source L *architectus* f. Gk *arkhitekton,* f. *arkhi-* **ARCHI-** + *tekton* builder.] **A** *n.* **1** A designer of buildings, who prepares plans, and superintends construction. M16. **b** In full *naval architect.* A designer of ships etc. M19. **2** A designer of any complex structure. L16. **3** A person who plans, devises, or contrives the achievement of a desired result. L16.

THE NEW SHORTER OXFORD ENGLISH DICTIONARY
ON HISTORICAL PRINCIPLES

EDITED BY
LESLEY BROWN

CLARENDON PRESS - OXFORD

1993

c In full software architect. A designer of software based technology, who prepares plans, and superintends construction

The
Software
Architect's
Profession

An Introduction

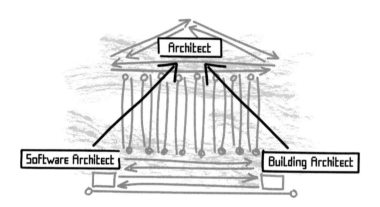

chapter 1

A Simple Analogy

*"All intelligent thoughts have already been
thought; what is necessary is only to try to
think them again."*[1]

Goethe

Ironically, it has been simple ideas—easily grasped—that have had the power to spark transformations of thought and knowledge. Throughout human history, we have seen simple concepts produce radical alterations of worldview. Freud posited the existence of a subconscious mind that motivated behavior; Copernicus's *De Revolutionibus* of 1530 proved the sun to be the center of the universe, and an apple falling on Newton's head was the catalyst for the train of thought leading to his Law of Gravitation.

These are preeminent examples, but simple "Aha!" experiences occur in our daily lives, as well. How many times does a solution evade us until we see the light and kick ourselves for not having seen the obvious—what was right under our noses from the start? Sometimes, the obvious comes to us in a dream. From time to time, entire groups of us are deluded until some kid shouts, "The emperor has no clothes!"

A *paradigm* is a model of thought, a different way of seeing something already seemingly familiar. Creating a new paradigm usually involves examining and challenging simple, underlying assumptions. This is not done by climbing up to the leaves and branches of existing thought; it happens when you dig down under the surface and get to the crucial *radix*—the root—of the tree, or the very way you have been seeing the tree.

The Perfect Analogy

There is a perfect, profound analogy between software and building construction. It is this analogy that is the simple idea that we have failed to see. From its inception, the software industry has been plagued by a crisis in the reliability, predictability, cost, and usability of its offerings. The industry has made continual advancements, certainly, but in the words of the English naturalist David Attenborough,

> "They grow by a series of moults but never... undergo transformation."[2]

With the application of the analogy, at all levels, the software industry can be transformed and elevated out of the mire of poor results and frustration. This analogy is not new, but it has never been fully explored or exploited. It has been used to make points, but it is often dismissed as too simplistic. In fact, the analogy holds true in all practical cases, simple and complex. Whether a structure is built of bricks, steel, or computer code, the roles and processes are analogous.

The analogy between software and building construction is far more than an academic exercise—it is an indispensable tool, a template. It is a touchstone in what has been a chaotic industry, and it provides clarity and predictability to our clients, software professionals, managers, and the "inhabitants" of our information systems. With the analogy, even nontechnical people can understand and validate the software construction process.

Finally, a Cognitive Map

When we move to a new town, we have difficulty navigating without the use of a map or directions. But soon we form a cognitive map and can drive anywhere with barely a conscious thought.

In the same way, through experience and observation, we all intuitively understand how buildings are constructed—from the most simple home to huge glass and steel towers. Even children have a cognitive map of the process and understand the differences between the roles of the architect, scientist, engineer, and builders. With the analogy, people will have the same mental image of how software is built. Everyone will know how the process begins, progresses, and when they can "move in," so to speak. They understand the roles of all involved. And people will see that, just like physical buildings, software can continue to be modified, renovated, and added to, even after the certificate of occupancy is signed.

Everyone also knows that buildings are created for shelter as well as to facilitate and enhance our multifarious activities. Kitchens are for cooking, bedrooms for sleeping, offices for working, and verandas for sitting on summer days. Museums house our precious legacies, and laundromats enable us to wash and dry our clothes. Buildings can be strictly utilitarian and dehumanizing—like our oversized mason block high schools—or structures of ineffable beauty. They can be cultural statements and even have a sense of humor, like the roadside stand in the shape of a hot dog.

With the analogy, people will similarly understand that software systems are extensions of our minds and form "rooms" for our multifarious activities. We have rooms for communication, or just plain chatting. We have libraries, stores, art studios, and places to do accounting and management. These sites can be utilitarian and dehumanizing or places of ineffable beauty. They can be as simple as a hut or as complex and finely detailed as the Alhambra. With this cognitive map, everyone can see that information systems are thoroughly analogous to physical buildings and will be able to think about those systems along the same familiar neural pathways.

With the clarity of the cognitive map, the analogy throws the light of day on how we have been constructing software. Overlaying the template of building construction on top of our software construction practices points the way to profound change.

With the analogy in mind, it swiftly becomes clear that an entire branch of knowledge has been missing from software construction. This branch of knowledge comprises one of the oldest professions in human history. The classical role of architecture and the architect has been largely absent from software construction and needs to be elevated and established. The software industry has been struggling without the discipline of true architectural design woven into its fabric.

It is time for this transformation to take place. Alvin Toffler wrote of history as a series of waves of transformation. The first wave came with the advent of agriculture. Humans ceased their

The Analogy Reveals the Missing Ingredient— Architecture

nomadic ways and were able to form stable villages that blossomed into modern societies. The second wave was ushered in by the Industrial Revolution. Machines replaced brute human and animal forces, and money supplanted land as the measure of wealth. We are now in the throes of transformation between the second and third waves—the Information Age—where knowledge is power.

It is noteworthy that the formal profession of software architecture is emerging on the crest of the third wave in a way similar to the establishment of the formal profession of building architecture on the crest of the second wave. In a profound sense, this is perfectly logical. New, complex physical structures were required to house and organize the numerous human activities created by the transformation from an agricultural to an industrial society. Professional architects with their own lexica and standards were needed to meet the demand in a reliable way.

The transformation to the third wave requires new, complex software structures to house and organize the human activities created by the transformation from an industrial age to an information age. Professional architects are needed to design these structures in a reliable way. New problems need to be solved on a large scale, and new types of structures need to be designed. We no longer have the luxury of building complex software structures without a design profession and without blueprints.

The Analogy Confers Clarity of Role and Purpose

When the CEO of IBM wanted a new corporate headquarters built, who did he call? A *"building scientist?"* A *"building engineer?"* A *"guru?"* Of course not. He called I. M. Pei—an *architect*. What would have happened if the Pope had never hired Michelangelo? Would St. Peter's Cathedral have *developed*? As it was, its design and construction were exceedingly difficult, and in the end, too many architects got their hands on it, but would it have been possible to even entertain such a vision as a basilica without an architect? Without a plan?

Unfortunately, there is no listing for software architects in the *Yellow Pages* and there are no I. M. Pei's in the industry—yet. The role of the architect has been missing along with the clear, classical roles for the client and the software builders. With the design role largely missing, a vacuum was created. This has been filled in by programmers, engineers, and computer scientists who do not have training and experience in design and who do not necessarily have an architectural worldview. In spite of this, they consider design to be a part of their role, but role confusion and muddled accountability are the result.

The book *Software Architecture in Practice*, by Bass, Clements, and Kazman, is illustrated throughout with a figure labeled the *"architect."* The book is about software *architecture* and is written, ostensibly, for software *architects*. But in their preface, the authors state the following:

"We are, after all, software engineers."[3]

Throughout the book, and throughout the industry, it is common for software professionals to refer to themselves as *architects* and *engineers* interchangeably. But with the analogy in place, titles, skills, and roles can finally become focused. We are not only confusing our clients with these ambiguities, we are also confusing ourselves.

Imagine you were building your dream home without a true architect, a blueprint, or clear roles for the engineer and builders. Imagine, in other words, building your home the way software is often built. You would likely begin by hiring a *building consultant* or *project manager*. In turn, they would bring in a number of people who would complete the requirements-gathering process. They would use an expensive requirements management package, and you would tell them everything you need in a home, how much money you could spend, and where it needs to be built. Your requirements would be very detailed, because you would have done your research:

Vulcan restaurant-style stove

Pecan-colored wood floors

Granite countertops in kitchen

High, coffered ceiling in great room

Tan marble in master bath

18 × 24-foot living room

Red brick exterior

Slate floor on the veranda

Four zones of heating and A/C

A warm, artistic look and feel

This list could be exhaustive, down to the wallpaper and carpet colors, and the brands of windows and door hardware.

The project manager would then hire a team of building specialists and building engineers. Meetings would ensue, and white boards would fill. The work would be divvied up among the groups until all requirements were accounted for. It would be decided that a bathroom, the kitchen, and a bedroom will be finished first, so the owner can save some money and move in faster. This would also show the owner how the rest of the house will look.

The roles of the builders would be decided according to their stated skills, experience, and toolboxes. It could be determined that the person completing a part of the electrical wiring would also hang the garage doors. The person laying the tile would also design the kitchen, having had some experience with that. The person doing a part of the plumbing, using the latest "copper pipe architectures," will be "architecting" the roof, as well, because that is where some of the plumbing vents lead. After all, we are all "building engineers."

The plan is to add to the finished rooms in a staged process, designing them ad hoc, until enough rooms exist on the site. There is a building specialist in charge of the interfaces between the rooms.

Anyone can see that this is a recipe for chaos. A house may result, yes, but what will it resemble? If it is dysfunctional, who's to blame? After all, the requirements have been met: The house has all the items specified by the owner. But does it work? As for the artistic look and feel, well, who can be artistic in a crisis?

It All Begins with a Client and an Architect

With the analogy, it is evident that all of those discrete requirements, even a 5-foot stack of them, do not cumulatively equal even a single sketch of an overall harmonious design for a house, a design whose process begins with the client and an architect. The client, in building construction, is not a mere *stakeholder*. The client plays a key, active role in building construction. Imagine Michelangelo referring to the Pope as a *stakeholder* or an *end-user*. The client owns the structure (either literally or figuratively) and works with the architect to form a *shared vision* of the final result—documented on a blueprint. The client then validates the construction as it proceeds.

The client can be wholly ignorant of flashings, bearing loads, footings, and building codes but can still validate that what is being built is true to the design. The tradesmen involved have their own lingo, methods, and tools, but the client does not need to learn them to remain in control of the project.

The architect and the plan form the bridge across the gulf between the client/users and the technical builders. The architect is always a client advocate, first and foremost, and intervenes on the client's behalf throughout the project. The architect has a foot in both worlds—the client's and the technical builder's. The architect understands both worlds and, in this way, is able to bring the intact design through the difficult construction phase.

Without the architect/advocate, a carpenter could tell the client, for example, that a desired curved staircase is impossible, given the space and angles at hand. The client would have to entertain several possibilities:

- Maybe this is the truth.
- Maybe the carpenter realized he lacks the skill or tools needed to build a curved staircase and does not want to admit this.
- Maybe the carpenter believes the staircase can't be built, when it really can.
- Maybe the carpenter underbid the job and decided the curved staircase is too expensive for the agreed-upon price.
- Maybe a more lucrative job is waiting, and the curves would be too time consuming.

The carpenter could use many technical terms in support of the argument—even geometric theorems—but the client, unless a skilled carpenter as well, would be unable to validate the truth. The owner's only way to settle all those "maybes" would be to hunt for a valid second opinion from another carpenter or construction consultant. Both those options are expensive in terms of fees, project delays, and the aggravation factor.

Now imagine this scenario with a trained, professional architect involved in the project. The carpenter would be unlikely to ever present an argument for a simpler staircase unless it truly was unfeasible or beyond his ken. And it is unlikely that the architect would have designed an unbuildable staircase in the first place. The architect could tell if the carpenter simply lacked the skill, or if there truly was a problem. In either case, the architect would determine the truth without the client's being put in such an untenable situation.

In the software field, however, builders rule the roost, and clients can seldom validate the design, process, cost, or outcome. Vision? Strategic use of technology? Design unity and elegance? Beautiful graphics? Clients can only hope the software structure will stand and not break the bank. But once the analogy is accepted and the classical role of the architect installed in the minds of people in the software industry, clarity of role and accountability will follow, cascading over to builders who will make the vision a reality.

By accepting the analogy, the software industry will be able to move toward a meaningful lexicon that mirrors the standardized terms used in building construction. E*ngineer* will mean *engineer*, not *architect*. Programmers will write code, the building blocks of software structures, not create *architectures*. We only mystify what we say when we use commonly understood words to mean wholly different things.

With the analogy, it is evident that the word *architecture* is synonymous with *design*. A*rchitecture* also refers to the field of architecture and its practice. A blueprint is not an architecture, and neither is an engineering element or an array of technical elements. The words *architecture* and *architectures* are widely misused in the software industry, confounding everyone. The analogy points the way to attaching meaningful words to these construction elements, as the building industry does. They use the actual names of things, such as joists, miter joints, circuit boxes, pipes, subwalls, circulators, and ground-fault outlets. These, or collections of these, are not architectures.

In the software industry, words have become the subject of great debate and controversy. These arguments are made all the more heated because the words in question are frequently divorced from clear, predictable processes and outcomes.

The following is a true story:

Meg is a manager for a large producer of agricultural products and was pleased to be assigned the role of overseer in the development of a new sales, inventory, shipping, and billing software system. A large consulting company was hired to build the system and they, in turn, hired many subcontractors.

As company project manager, Meg worked closely with the project manager from the consulting firm—an experienced technical person who had worked on many software development projects. He had a sophisticated project plan and precise time lines developed with the help of a project management tool. But in spite of this, expenses started to climb rather alarmingly.

Meg wondered if she just didn't have enough technical background to understand what the problem was. The requirements documentation was meticulous, and the project plan was as detailed as imaginable. But control was slipping away from her.

She decided to hold a meeting with the two highest level technical people on the project—people with exemplary resumes in the industry. They were the gurus and could tell her where things were going wrong. But instead of providing answers, the technical experts argued heatedly for more than an hour over the meaning of the terms analysis-level design *and* low-level design*. One contended that there* *was little distinction and that both levels should exist on one document. The other stubbornly insisted that there was a profound difference and two documents were needed.*

This intense interchange created a surge of panic in Meg, who had the classic epiphany that "the inmates are running the asylum." She wondered how they could be arguing over design documents when the programmers were actually coding. What were they building?

The technical leads were obviously brilliant people. She was quite brilliant as well. How could this be happening, she wondered. She totally understood the business need and had a complete mental image of the product she needed. She heard the meter ticking at the rate of $2,000 a day, each, for these people, and not only could they not converge on a design, they also couldn't agree on what design was—and the project had been under way for three months.

Meg left the conference room, trying hard to hang on to her composure.

The argument over words in this counterproductive scenario was also an argument over the process. If the processes were predictable, as they are in building construction, it really would not have mattered what the document was called. There would have been a blueprint containing a joint understanding of the design, and the name of it would have been irrelevant. It doesn't matter to building professionals if a home is said to have a Southwestern *style*, *architecture*, or *design*. The process and roles are the same, and the house—well, it speaks for itself.

"Design it first and then carefully build it" sounds like an adage that overstates the obvious, but it is one that does not apply predictably to the construction of software. There is a logical order to design and construction processes in building construction that needs to be used as a template in the software industry.

With the Analogy, Processes Are Predictable

The process begins with the client and architect who converge on an architectural plan. Once the design phase is complete, the client can see the building and its entire organization in the form of a blueprint, 3-D model, or both. The engineer, inspector, builder, interior designer, plumber, electrician, and carpenter—everyone with a role in the construction process—then use the same plan for different purposes.

The architect's plan, or blueprint, is the high-level design, but during construction, the builders design as well. For example, the architectural plan could indicate the placement of electrical outlets and light fixtures, the number of telephone circuits, and even the requirement that the circuits be "home runs" without splices. The plan could also detail the brand, style, and even part number of light fixtures, outlets, and switches.

The master electrician, in turn, would design the circuit boxes and the general layout of the wiring. Indeed, it would be up to the electrician to design anything not specifically detailed by the architect, such as the type of wire, circuit breakers, and so forth. This is *low-level design*—but it doesn't stop there.

The electrician's helper, in turn, might design the way the wires run through the rafters and down the inside of the walls. Just as the master electrician designed anything not included in the architectural plan, the helper designs anything not specifically addressed by the master electrician. And each level of design is supervised by the person at the next higher level.

This orderly process is so ingrained in the building construction process that it does not require articulation. It is the industry standard and the expectation of all involved. It does not prevent flexibility or complexity—it actually allows them to flourish, because the builders are not bogged down by confused processes, roles, and accountabilities.

The roles of the scientists and engineers are equally clear. Scientists conduct research and further the field of building materials, tools, and methods. Engineers work with architects and builders to ensure that the structure can be built as designed and will be strong enough to meet demands.

The Analogy Brings Order to Complexity and Flexibility

The root cause of software failure and inefficiency is not attributable to the complex nature of software technology but to the rather prosaic, human reason that we have failed to build software as we build buildings. The analogy has been used in the software industry in a limited way merely to illustrate points or raise questions, but it has never been pushed far enough. It has been dismissed as too simplistic, but perhaps complexity is being confused with chaos.

Critics have been too quick to reject the analogy. Buildings, when you think about it, are exceedingly complex. There is an entire body of scientific research on methods, tools, and materials. A simple piece of plywood is the culmination of years of continuous testing and improvement in laminates, woods, glues, and manufacturing methods. Electricians have a hierarchy all their own and bask in lingo. Great plumbers regard a complex network of copper piping as a work of art—and rightly so. It takes absolutely no special training to live in a house, appreciate it, or even keep it clean and functioning, but intensive research and development backs up the myriad of systems contained in even small structures. Skyscrapers are another matter entirely.

It defies logic to suggest that building technology is simplistic. Engineering and design feats accomplished by the human race span the centuries, from the pyramids to the cathedrals to the Sears Tower. Building construction seems simplistic only because an orderly, systematic process, clear roles, and clear plans manage the complexity.

In a similar vein, don't assume that the analogy limits flexibility, because there is great flexibility inherent in building construction. There are times, for example, when a building architect isn't hired at all. Perhaps a simple structure is being built, or the builder may decide to use a set of blueprints from a magazine. A skilled builder may be able to construct a garage or room addition with just sketches. Much depends on the individual skill and experience of the builder and the task at hand, but, even in these cases, the design comes first, is validated by the client, and is bid on by the contractors before ground is ever broken. From there, the roles and skill sets of the builders are predictable.

There is flexibility, too, for both buildings and software to evolve and improve over time. Maybe a client can afford only a basic house plan to start, leaving large elements remaining to be completed at a later time—such as a garage, guest room, or pool. However, it is vital that these architectural elements be considered up front in the architectural design.

The architect plans for those elements in many ways: The proper space must be allowed for them on the site plan; building codes and variances must be known and met; the floor plan needs to be conducive to these future elements to "work"; and the installation of utilities must be taken into account. If these steps are not taken, the garage, pool, or addition may never happen at all or may require a major redesign of all or part of the existing structure.

Contrast this organized approach with that of the software industry. Have you seen software projects where design was done ad hoc, concurrently with construction? Where a representation of a high-level design outlining the true scope, organization, and behaviors of an information system did not exist, was incomplete, or was not followed? Or where the client did not understand or was surprised by the final result? Or where future needs for flexibility or expansion were not integrated into the initial construction and a part of the overall plan?

Conclusion

The elemental force of the analogy will not only lead to the establishment of a true profession of software architecture, but it also will have far-reaching ripple effects. It will transform the way software is built by clarifying the roles and accountabilities of software professionals, introducing predictable, orderly processes, and standardizing the lexicon. Most stunningly, the analogy will allow clients and "inhabitants" of software systems to assume their rightful place as the owners and managers of information technology systems, as surely as residents supervise the construction and maintenance of their own homes.

Endnotes

1. Johann Wolfgang von Goethe, *Proverbs in Prose*, translated by Norbert Guterman, in *Familiar Quotations*, 16th ed., ed. Justin Kaplan. (Boston: Little, Brown & Co., 1992), 351.

2. David Attenborough, in *The New Shorter Oxford English Dictionary*, Thumb Index ed. (Oxford: Oxford University Press, 1993), 3369.

3. Len Bass, Paul Clements, and Rick Kazman, *Software Architecture in Practice* (Reading, Mass.: Addison-Wesley, 1998), xi.

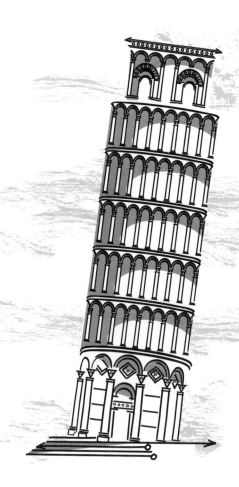

chapter 2

A World Without Architects

*"The lack of usability of software and the
poor design of programs is the secret
shame of the industry."*[1]

Mitchell Kapor, 1990

Know this: If software and information technology systems were suddenly visible as physical buildings, of a size commensurate with their costs, the phrase "software crisis" would pepper the headlines. Perceptible to all would be a landscape strewn with vacant, unfinished structures—some the size of skyscrapers—lying useless and abandoned by the side of the road. There would be functional buildings, too, but with empty rooms, dead spaces, and unhappy inhabitants.

Neighboring these inefficient buildings and exquisitely expensive failures, in a scene worthy of Jonathan Swift, we would witness similar buildings being erected by the same construction companies and crews responsible for the empty fiascoes. The builders would be brandishing new tools and sagely offering scary new lingo, as they and their clients harbored the naïve hope that the utter resourcefulness of Homo constructivus would lead, this time, to success.

Unfortunately, though, builders of software continue to produce results that fail to meet expectations, or fail completely, despite increasingly sophisticated tools and methodologies. The poor, forgotten clients continue to pay for these efforts, often asking themselves: "What is a methodology, anyway?"

The Paradox of the Software Industry

The software professionals who build failed structures bear a heavy burden. They deny themselves the satisfaction of producing results that meet or exceed the expectations of clients and, at times, must live with the knowledge that what they created is never even used. In this respect, there is a stunning paradox central to their lives. On the one hand, they work in an industry caught in the whirlwind of innovation. Software is embedded in everything from pacemakers to pickup trucks, and just keeping in pace with technological advancements and changes in human patterns of communication and decision making is a do-or-die proposition for many businesses. You are either the quick or the dead. Information systems are more than a way to track and manipulate data; they have become critical success factors in the Darwinian realm of business.

On the other side of the paradox, software professionals live with the wholly different reality that lies beyond the view of the media and general public. These professionals live with what is commonly referred to as the "software crisis." The unrealized Y2K crisis pierced the public consciousness with its "millennium fever" cachet, but the real software crisis, while largely invisible to the popular culture, is not a false alarm.

Within the software industry, the term *software crisis* is all too familiar—even a cliché cast aside. It was coined in 1968 and continues to be mentioned in book after book and paper after paper, because the solution is so elusive. Entire books document software failure, chaos, and general dissatisfaction, such as Robert Glass's *Computing Calamities*, Alan Cooper's *The Inmates are Running the Asylum*, and Robert L. Glass's *Software Runaways*.

Grady Booch, author of the authoritative book on software development, *Object Solutions: Managing the Object-Oriented Project*, admits

> I was tempted to name this book *Projects in Crisis*, because it seems that every interesting project of reasonable complexity is a project in crisis, no matter what its technology base. . . .[2]

Everyone in the software industry has favorite anecdotes about project failures, although no one involved ever seems to know how to apportion the blame. But something is very wrong, indeed. The Standish Group found that the chance of a software project developed by a Fortune 500 company coming in on time and within budget was only 23.6 percent. A much higher percentage, estimated to be as high as 40 percent, is cancelled before completion. The remainder are either significantly challenged or, if successful, over budget and behind schedule.

The March of the Notorious

Trend data is helpful in analyzing the scope and nature of software failure but, as usual, the details are where the demons dwell. Case studies of software development failures expose details, but they are hard to find for the simple reason that private businesses do not willingly advertise their weaknesses. And because software exists in the abstract, you can't watch it being scrapped as you can a building torn down by a wrecking ball.

Instead, failed code and towers of documentation are quietly relegated to the corporate dumpster, and the company hobbles along with subpar systems, making the best of things. Shareholders and the public are none the wiser as these companies and their software contractors strive to put their best foot forward.

Fortunately, the U.S. government is an entity of, for, and by the people. As such, American citizens are the ones who footed the bill for several behemoth software debacles. To our benefit, the culpable public servants and contractors have had no place to hide when called on the carpet before Congress. Their detailed testimony has given some of the best insights into the world without architects.

No resources were spared in these government projects. The government spent unfathomable sums on technology and the very best blue-chip contractors, but still the projects failed.

The Federal Aviation Administration

The Federal Aviation Administration (FAA) began its massive revamping of the entire air traffic control system in 1982, projecting that it would take 11 years to complete. It began with a four-year design competition eventually won by IBM. The goal was to modernize the entire air traffic control system, but much of the effort—and many of the problems—centered on the development of the individual air traffic controller workstations. The controllers' radarscopes were to be replaced with a mainframe-based network. The reliability requirement was daunting: The network had to be up and operational 99.9999 percent of the time, with no ability to bring down the system to fix bugs.

Incomplete or ever-changing customer requirements often are blamed for project failure, including this one, but in this case, it would be hard to imagine a greater degree of requirements precision. The stacked specification documents were said to be 20 feet high.

It is difficult to accurately describe the intensive, disciplined management approach IBM and the FAA brought to bear on the development effort. Meeting protocols were strictly regimented, as were inspections and quality assurance measures. Over 2,000 IBM'ers were working on the software at the peak of the development effort, in addition to FAA employees and subcontractors.

IBM delivered a new workstation after many delays, but it never was implemented. There were some very basic problems. Despite all the requirements gathering, air traffic controllers themselves were not consulted regarding the design and prototyping. It was believed that to do so would inhibit the development of truly innovative technical solutions. So it was learned after the fact that the workstation software pulled the human air traffic controller's attention away from the task of tracking individual aircraft for unsafe intervals of time.

Instead of being able to turn a knob by touch to create an airplane's vector line, for example, the controller would have to enter 16 keystrokes. Also, the electronically created tracking strips generated for each aircraft kept falling into the controllers' laps.

These were not the only problems, but they are prime examples. In addition, the project was just too ambitious—there was just too much invention attempted at one time, when an "encapsulate and conquer" strategy should have been undertaken to implement so many innovations.

How could this have happened? How could a collective of elite minds—a veritable brain trust—fail in such an ordinary way?

The air traffic controllers' union complained about the lack of input from the controllers, and rightly so. The task of the controller is an intricate combination of sight, sound, spatial relationships, decision making, and perceptual patterns. Changing controllers' software without detailed consultation defies sense. Most certainly, the software developers asked the controllers for their requirements, but obviously they never reached a true meeting of the minds, a true understanding. It is also clear that the controllers never had the opportunity to *validate* what was being built for them, either before or during construction, despite an entire room of requirements documentation.

In 1997, the General Accounting Office published a post-mortem report detailing their analysis of the problem and recommendation for modernizing the FAA. It is titled "Air Traffic Control: Complete and Enforced **Architecture** Needed for FAA Systems Modernization" (emphasis added).

In the end, it was evident that the FAA attempted to build an information skyscraper from lists of requirements and specifications, but without architects and without an architectural design understandable and verifiable by the clients. Many critics of the project blamed "changing requirements" for the debacle, but the requirements churned ceaselessly because the design was never right to begin with. There is no architecture discipline, no body of architectural knowledge, in the software industry, and the FAA (and American citizens) suffered as a result.

It was admirable that the FAA began the process with a design competition, but the four years it took seems too long considering that prototyping was not done during the design phase. When so many high-risk inventions are being proposed, prototyping needs to be done in the design phase. Indeed, the FAA and IBM missed the entire point of an architectural design phase. It is the time for the client and the "inhabitants" to verify that the design is correct. Are they satisfied? Do they understand the design? If not, how can we model it, draw it, and prototype it in a way they do understand?

What happened is analogous to hiring an army of technicians and construction workers to build a skyscraper on East 34th Street in New York City with 120 floors. The stacks of requirements could fill rooms—as the FAA requirements did—and heroic management controls could be put in place to regulate their minute-by-minute activities. But does that mean that the resulting structure would even resemble the Empire State Building?

By some accounts, the IRS TSM failure cost U.S. taxpayers $3.3 billion dollars. Others, including the firm of Deloitte & Touche, peg the figure at around $8 billion. In either case, to put the magnitude into perspective, it would take the citizens of a midsized American town like Kennesaw, Georgia, or Weehawken, New Jersey, several centuries of hard-earned tax dollars to pay for this largely scrapped project.

The IRS TSM began as an amalgam of good ideas, including a central goal of implementing optical scanners to take the place of manual data input. On the surface it would be hard to disagree with the logic of this technology, but in reality, after millions had

Internal Revenue Service Tax System Modernization (TSM)

A World Without Architects

been invested in scanners, they couldn't even get the 1040EZ implemented. The scanners were only about 95 percent accurate in their character recognition, and they could scan only one side of the page at a time.

It is overstating the obvious to point out that a 5 percent error rate is catastrophic when processing millions of tax returns, and that the back of the document is important too, even when it contains only a worksheet. After a tremendous investment, the IRS legal staff determined that, yes, the back of the document was legally necessary to complete the taxpayer's return. It taxes the mind to try to figure out how they couldn't have known that ahead of time—but they simply didn't. No one was accountable for such design points.

The misapplication of scanner technology was only part of the problem. The IRS had a critical shortage of the "intellectual capital" needed for such a complex project, which was led by business managers, not technical experts. The technical people they did have developing software were organized (or, rather, not organized) on

> ...many large and somewhat unrelated projects [that] have been gathered into one gargantuan collection that the IRS calls TSM.[3]

The General Accounting Office (GAO) and the National Academy of Sciences postmortem reports called for the immediate hiring of a highly qualified CIO—along with a technical leadership team, of course—but then their first recommendation called for an architectural design:

> Despite almost a decade of activity, the architectural design of TSM either is nonexistent or is hidden in a forest of detail. The IRS must develop a complete, concise architectural definition that can be used by the almost 2,000 IRS developers and their contractors.
>
> An architecture is more than just a set of documents with many words and pictures. An architecture also includes the critical pieces needed to analyze parts of the system before it is built or while it is being prototyped. Such analysis is critical to the ultimate success of a large system. . . .
>
> There is no substitute for an adequate architectural definition and system model. If the IRS does not address this soon, some very large investments may never yield significant benefits.[4]

The National Academy of Sciences (NAS) and GAO went on to say that although the IRS developed volumes of software-planning documents, there was still no discernable architecture, and

> …no single document that concisely states the overall requirements and specifications and that thus would allow an outside technologist, as well as the many IRS technologists involved, to understand the system structure of TSM. Such a document is needed as a basis for all design and development decisions and, as such, is critical to the success of TSM.[5]

An independent Office of Chief Architect was proposed to design and develop the blueprint that would then be subject to the scrutiny of the IRS and the private sector before development continued on TSM. Once again, as was the case with the FAA and the thousands of failing and ailing software systems in all sectors, the builders were constructing without an architectural plan.

Or, as John Ruskin said so incisively in 1880:

> for I believe that failure is less frequently attributable to either insufficiency of means or impatience of labour, than to a confused understanding of the thing actually to be done.[6]

Blaming software failure or difficulty on "changing requirements" is merely symptomatic of the lack of true architecture. When the owners and builders see what is being built, they realize that it is wrong and start to make changes in a post hoc attempt to bring the reality of the structure in line with their expectations.

It is equally erroneous to blame software failure on poor management. Without a profession of architecture, it is the design that is missing. Even the best managers cannot produce a satisfying result from a bad design or the lack of design. And management cannot compensate for the lack of a standardized construction process, vague roles, and confusing lexica. Only skilled architects, in partnership with their clients, can design "the thing actually to be done." The MBAs call it *business process reengineering*. We call it *architecture*.

Frederick P. Brooks, in the Twentieth Anniversary Edition of his classic computing book *The Mythical Man-Month*, concludes

> Today I am more convinced than ever. Conceptual integrity *is* central to product quality. Having a system architect *is* the most important single step toward conceptual integrity. These principles are by no means limited to software systems, but to the design of any complex construct, whether a computer, an airplane, a Strategic Defense Initiative, a Global Positioning System.[7]

Conclusion

The FAA and IRS are really just the celebrities leading a miles-long parade of failures and half-failures that has grown over the years as a result of a world without an established profession of software architecture. The wasted money and intellectual resources are staggering, but even greater: The software crisis has impeded the full flowering of the Information Age.

Alvin Toffler calls it the third wave, but whatever the rubric, the phenomenon represents the transformation of our world through information technology. It cannot be realized without true architects.

Endnotes

1. Mitchell Kapor, "A Software Design Manifesto," *Bringing Design to Software*, ed. Terry Winograd (Reading, Mass.: ACM Press/Addison-Wesley, 1996), 3.

2. Grady Booch, *Object Solutions: Managing the Object-Oriented Project* (Menlo Park, Calif.: Addison-Wesley, 1996), 119.

3. National Academy of Sciences, "Continued Review of the Tax System Modernization of the Internal Revenue Service," 1996.

4. Ibid.

5. Ibid.

6. John Ruskin, *The Seven Lamps of Architecture* (New York: Dover Publications, 1989), 1.

7. Frederick P. Brooks, *The Mythical Man-Month*, Anniversary ed. (Reading, Mass.: Addison-Wesley, 1995), 257.

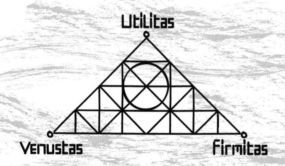

chapter 3

What Is Architecture?

"The happy towns are those that have an architecture."[1]

"Architecture can be found in the telephone and in the Parthenon. How easily could it be at home in our houses!"[2]

"Architecture is the first manifestation of man creating his own universe, creating it in the image of nature, submitting to the laws of nature, the laws which govern our own nature, our universe. The laws of gravity, of statics and of dynamics, impose themselves by a reductio ad absurdum: *everything must hold together or it will collapse."*[3]

"Architecture has nothing to do with the various 'styles.' The styles of Louis XIV, XV, XVI or Gothic, are to architecture what a feather is on a woman's head; it is sometimes pretty, though not always, and never anything more."[4]

Le Corbusier

The profession of architecture has been missing from the software industry, but the first step in establishing it is to attempt to understand the essential nature of architecture, as it has existed throughout human history. Words should have clear meanings but, unfortunately, in the field of information technology, words, titles, and roles are muddled and confused. Anyone can call himself or herself an architect, "blueprints" detail processes and activities rather than a design, and other common words have multiple meanings. It is ironic that this is the case in a field where precision would be expected as a dominant character trait, but it has become common for software professionals to bandy about words such as *architect, designer, architectures, styles,* and *models* without using their commonly held meanings.

It is critical for information technology professionals and their clients to know what architecture is. It is far more than "technical architectures" (akin to the layout of pipes or wires), the mapping of a domain, or a series of protocols. In order for the analogy to make sense and the profession of software architecture to be a reality, we have to ask and try to answer the question: What is the essential nature of architecture, as it has always existed? Only when this is understood can we apply the true concept of architecture to the world of software-based technology.

Is architecture, for example, just artistic style applied to structures? Is it design? Building architecture is all around us; we cannot avoid it—as we can avoid even art and music—and we all know what it is on a certain level, yet the word *architecture* is conceptual and defies precise definition. Entire books have been written just to ask and explore the question, "What is architecture?" This is a striking fact given that architecture is as old as recorded history, yet the answer to the question never gets closer than an approximation of the truth, like Plato's shadows on the wall.

It helps to remember that architecture, the grand concept, is separate from the applied activity and the products of architecture, such as buildings, software structures, and boats. The same is true of art, a thoroughly indefinable concept, but one that finds physical form in paintings, sculptures, and performances.

> ...architecture really does not exist. Only a work of architecture exists. Architecture does exist in the mind. A man who does a work of architecture does it as an offering to the spirit of architecture...a spirit which knows no style, knows no technique, no method. It just waits for that which presents itself. There is architecture, and it is the embodiment of the unmeasurable.[5]
>
> Louis Kahn

There are many interpretations of architecture and theory in books, but

> Going into a stack of books in pursuit of architecture is like looking in a butcher's shop for a sheep; it's there all right, but laid out in a rather particular way.[6]
>
> Paul Shepheard

For our purposes in regard to software, it is a substantial first step to know that architecture is not a narrow concept referring only to building design, and it never has been. In fact, it has held broader meanings in the past, both direct and allegorical, than it does today. In reality, the relationship between building and software architecture is more than an illustrative analogy since architecture has always been broad enough to include a structure such as an information technology system as a part of itself. Building and software architecture are branches growing from the same trunk of *architecture*. Both are true architecture, and software architecture should not be regarded as just an analogy. It *is* architecture.

Vitruvius was an architect who lived during the era of the Roman Empire. He has become a founding father of architecture and is the author of the ten books of architecture, De *Architectura*. Much of Western architectural theory has flowed from his genius. Vitruvius wrote that architecture applies to three categories: buildings, machines, and timepieces (by which he meant sundials). The machines he alluded to were the Roman models used to break down the defenses of city walls. Michelangelo, too, was an architect of modern warfare devices for the Italian city-state of Florence, at a much later time.

Technology— The Common Thread of Architecture

So even the earliest concepts of architecture were broad and technology-focused. Architecture can be seen as a body of knowledge—a design discipline—applied to branches of technology. This technological underpinning of architecture is a common thread joining the branches of architecture: buildings, machines, timepieces, ships, and now software. In this key respect, software architecture is positively Vitruvian in spirit, and it is fairly safe (although maybe presumptuous) to believe that Vitruvius would have endorsed the analogy.

Everyone enjoys trying to pin down the elusive. John Ruskin defined architecture in 1874 (rather metaphysically) as the adaptation of form to resist force, while Goethe in 1829 called architecture "frozen music." Sallust, a contemporary of Vitruvius's, wrote that every man is the architect of his own fortune; Milton wrote of those who were the architects of their own happiness; and Robert Browning wrote

Many Definitions of the Indefinable

> That far land we dream about,
> Where every man is his own architect.

Red Cotton Nightcap Country (1873)

As for the definitive, so to speak, definition of architecture, *The New Shorter Oxford English Dictionary* offers this:

architecture /'a:kitEktSer /n.&v. M16. [Fr., or L *architectura*: see ARCHITECT, -URE.] **A** *n*. **1** The art or science of building; *esp*. the art or practice of designing and building edifices for human use, taking both aesthetic and practical factors into account. M16 **2** Architectural work;

something built. L16. **3** A style of building; mode, manner, or style of construction or organization; structure. E17. **B** The conceptual structure and logical organization of a computer or computer-based system. M20. **4** The action or process of building; construction. *arch.* E17.

I marine architecture, naval architecture the design and building of ships etc.[7]

So architecture is architecture is architecture, regardless of the nature and purpose of the designed structure. It is not poetic license or a convenient theoretical posture to propose the analogy with software. The broad meaning of architecture has been accepted for centuries, and even the writers of the *Oxford Dictionary* accept software architecture as a subset of architecture.

Utilitas, Venustas, Firmitas

Vitruvius wrote that all architecture is comprised of the elements of function, beauty, and structure. This triad has formed the basis of architecture since ancient Rome and has the simple elegance to form the theoretical basis of software architecture, as well. James O'Gorman has written cogently on the Vitruvian triad:

> Architects think geometrically, and so must we. Envision Vitruvius's definition as an equilateral triangle with one of his factors at each corner. Each is discrete, yet all combine to shape a larger whole. That larger whole, represented by our equilateral triangle, is the work of architecture.[8]

Utilitas represents the need for a structure—the function of the structure. This side of the triangle is the perspective of the client and inhabitants who, whatever the motivation, perceive an unmet need that can be met through a building or software construction program. Some clients see their need as a problem to be solved—such as a dysfunctional order entry system that slows productivity and impedes customer service. Other clients see the need as an opportunity to increase profit or market share, such as an airline that can gain a competitive advantage through a better mileage reward system. Still other clients may see the need as a way to better service their customers, students, or the citizens they serve. *Utilitas* is the reason or desire for a building project and the function it will serve. This is the role of the client.

Venustas is the design. The design is created to meet the functional need of the client and represents the organization and artistic arrangement of the systems and materials. This is the role and responsibility of the architect.

Firmitas represents the means, materials, and logistics of construction. Without a solid, well-built structure, the need of the client is not met and the design is never realized. *Firmitas* is the role of the builders.

Within this triad, there are ancillary roles such as those of engineers, consultants, and managers. These roles are necessary adjuncts and are subsumed by the primary triad of function, design, and construction. The engineer, for example, is typically hired by the architect to certify the strength of structural elements. The engineer may also be hired by a builder in need of expertise in how to build a certain element.

The Vitruvian triad translates perfectly to software construction and is an elegant cognitive map of the essential roles and responsibilities engaged in the creation of a structure.

The Mystery of Design

Structures are conceptualized and realized through the triad of function, design, and construction, but the result can range from the ridiculous to the sublime. Great design—design that meets the needs of the inhabitants and is aesthetically pleasing—has been the subject of many fine books and is a field of study unto itself.

Great design is the *raison d'être* of architects, yet in the software field, it rarely has been mentioned. There are software professionals who do not think a system's design needs to be documented at all; that it is sufficient to let it evolve through the building process, remaining forever implicit. Others see software architecture and design as just a phase rather than the critical activity it is. As Peter Freeman explains:

> In general, it is wise to concentrate time and resources on the analysis and design activities, since a dollar spent there will often be worth ten or a hundred dollars spent later. The reason for that has been presented repeatedly in the literature and comes down to the simple fact that as in most things, understanding a problem and planning a solution, if done carefully, will help prevent mistakes during construction or operation that are very difficult and costly to fix. Additionally, there are critical properties of software, such as reliability, that cannot be added on to a system during construction; they must be *designed* in.[9]

It is our hope that besides lowering the astoundingly high rates of software project failure, the establishment of a true profession of software architecture will lead to glorious design. It is also hoped that there will be design competitions, juries, and a software architecture critic at *The New York Times*. Great design results from the architect's understanding of the client's world, as well as architectural vision and skill; it does not emerge from committees or the collective efforts of builders. It does not grow from casual regard or from the hands of those who see design as a piecemeal development phase.

The Lesson of St. Peter's: Harmony and Unity

The classic legacies of building architecture hold many profound lessons for software architects. St. Peter's Basilica is famous and grand, but it suffered when competing visions were inflicted upon the design.

Michelangelo, almost superhuman in his inventiveness and aliveness, was the architect commissioned by the Pope to design a cathedral dedicated to St. Peter, the apostle to whom Jesus said, "Upon this rock I build my church." Michelangelo was 72 years old at the time and all his life he really just wanted to be a sculptor. But his client, the Pope, was always able to talk him into doing things like paintings, buildings, and tombs.

Michelangelo had tried unsuccessfully to foist the Sistine Chapel assignment off on Raphael at an earlier time, but he now devoted himself to the design of St. Peter's until his death at the age of 89. Subsequently, popes and architects couldn't resist making their marks upon the ongoing project—killing the vision and quality of the design.

Here, Le Corbusier speaks to the lesson of Rome and St. Peter's, and to us about the soul of architectural unity and harmony:

> The dimensions are considerable. To construct such a dome in stone was a *tour de force* that few men would have dared. ...The general arrangement of the apses and of the Attic storey is allied to that of the Colosseum; the heights are the same. The whole scheme was a complete unity; it grouped together elements of the noblest and richest kind: the Portico, the cylinders, the square shapes, the drum, the dome. The mouldings are of an intensely *passionate* character, harsh and pathetic. The whole design would have risen as a single mass, unique and entire. The eye would have taken it in as one thing. Michael Angelo completed the apses and the drum of the dome. The rest fell into barbarian hands; all was spoilt. Mankind lost one of the highest works of human intelligence. If one can imagine Michael Angelo as cognizant of the disaster, we have a terrifying drama.[10]

One of the barbarians was Bernini, as Le Corbusier explains:

> Verbose and awkward. Bernini's Colonnade is beautiful in itself. The façade is beautiful in itself, but bears no relation to the Dome. The real aim of the building was the Dome; it has been hidden! The Dome was in a proper relation to the apses: they

have been hidden. The Portico was a solid mass: it has become merely a front.[11]

...foolish and thoughtless Popes dismissed Michael Angelo; miserable men have murdered St. Peter's within and without. It has become stupidly enough the St. Peter's of to-day, like a rich and pushing cardinal, lacking...*everything*. Immense loss! A passion, an intelligence beyond normal—this was the Everlasting Yea; it has become sadly enough a "perhaps," an "apparently," an "it may be," an "I am not sure." Wretched failure![12]

The lesson of Rome is for wise men, for those who know and can appreciate, who can resist and can verify. Rome is the damnation of the half-educated. To send architectural students to Rome is to cripple them for life.[13]

Le Corbusier's passion for elegant design is contagious, and the lessons are great for software architects. The abstract, invisible nature of software is used to hide poor design from clients and end-users, and it is made even more invisible by the lack of explicit blueprints so rampant in the industry. But the user of a software system experiences the same sense of "rightness" or "wrongness" in response to poor or discordant design as a building occupant does. And just as a person with an unpracticed eye might find St. Peter's beautiful, so would a naïve, unstudied software user find an awkward system satisfactory.

The Quality Without a Name

There is a central quality which is the root criterion of life and spirit in a man, a town, a building, or a wilderness. This quality is objective and precise, but it cannot be named.

The search which we make for this quality, in our own lives, is the central search of any person, and the crux of any individual person's story. It is the search for those moments and situations when we are most alive.[14]

Christopher Alexander

Both software users and building occupants experience that sense of rightness or wrongness and often have difficulty articulating exactly why. "I just like it" is a perfectly acceptable answer and high praise. Christopher Alexander, a brilliant building architect from Berkeley, California, describes this ineffable "quality without a name" in *The Timeless Way of Building*. It lies at the heart of the questions "What is good architecture?" and "What is good design?"

The quality without a name is experienced rather than voiced and can be a part of a building, a person, a part of a software application, a piece of music, a town—anything. A tenet of Mr. Alexander's philosophy is based on patterns: Our lives are patterns of events, done over and over again; a town evolves according to the human patterns of its inhabitants; a building is a collection of design patterns that either bring the occupants to life or thwart them. Good architecture, good design, must be congruent with our individual and collective patterns of behavior and perception.

> Consider two human patterns. On the one hand, consider the fact that certain Greek village streets have a band of whitewash, four or five feet wide, outside every house, so that people can pull their chairs out into the street, into a realm which is half theirs, half street, and so contribute to the life around them.
>
> And on the other hand, consider the fact that cafes in Los Angeles are indoors, away from the sidewalk, in order to prevent food from being contaminated.
>
> Both these patterns have a purpose. One has the purpose of allowing people to contribute to the street life and to be part of it—to the extent they desire—by marking a domain which makes it possible. The other has the purpose of keeping people healthy, by making sure that they will not eat food that has dust particles on it. Yet one is alive; the other dead.[15]

Mr. Alexander further explains that the Greek pattern of whitewash sustains itself. The occupants freshen it each year willingly, because it is a pattern they connect to and value. The indoor cafes, on the other hand, can be sustained only by force of law:

> People want to be outdoors on a spring day, want to drink their beer or coffee in the open, to watch the world go by, but they are imprisoned in the café by the laws of public health. The situation is self-destroying, not only because it will change as soon as the law which upholds it disappears, but also in the more subtle sense that it is continuously creating just those inner conflicts, just those reservoirs of stress...which will, unsatisfied, soon well up like a gigantic boil and leak out in some other form of destruction or refusal to cooperate with the situation.[16]

This is but one fine example of Christopher Alexander's ideas regarding architectural patterns, but it perfectly illustrates the natural, human aesthetics that mysteriously and inexorably lead us to feel more, or less, alive. These inner dictates lie at the heart of great design and are profoundly important to the profession of software architecture.

Conclusion

What is software but simply metaphorical rooms, buildings, and towns made up of human patterns of behavior and perception? There are happy applications that are a pleasure to use, acquiring self-sustaining lives of their own, and others that lead inhabitants to throw equipment from windows. There is software that invokes the magical feeling of a veranda where you lose track of time and feel intensely alive. Software is subject to the same aesthetic principles as structures from our architectural past and will require the same application of fine design to elevate it beyond the mundane.

We need to see that only the products of architecture vary: buildings, software, ships, machines, and timepieces—even our own fates. The materials are widely divergent—wood, steel, computer code—and these materials drive vastly different techniques and trades. But all the products of architecture belong to *homo constructivus*, who creates structures to extend and enhance human activity beyond itself. These products of architecture are technology-focused and are realized through the interdependent triad of utilitas, venustas, and firmitas.

The profession of software architecture has been missing from software construction and needs to be established. Only a true discipline of software architecture, consistent with the classical concept of architecture, will elevate software to stand on par with the great architectural legacies of the past.

Endnotes

1. Le Corbusier, *Toward a New Architecture* (Mineola, N.Y.: Dover Publications, 1986), 15.

2. Ibid., 15.

3. Ibid., 73.

4. Ibid., 37.

5. Louis Kahn, in *Louis Kahn: Writings, Lectures, Interviews*, ed. Alessandra Latour (New York: Rizzoli International Publications, 1991), 168.

6. Paul Shepheard, *What Is Architecture? An Essay on Landscapes, Buildings, and Machines* (Cambridge, Mass.: The MIT Press, 1994), 25.

7. Lesley Brown, editor, *The New Shorter Oxford English Dictionary on Historic Principles* (Oxford: Clarendon Press, 1993).

8. James O'Gorman, *ABC of Architecture* (Philadelphia, Pa.: University of Pennsylvania Press, 1998), 10.

9. Peter Freeman, *Software Perspectives: The System Is the Message* (Reading, Mass.: Addison-Wesley Publishing, 1987), 148.

10. Le Corbusier, Ibid., 170.

12. Ibid., 171.

13. Ibid., 172.

14. Ibid., 173.

14. Christopher Alexander, *The Timeless Way of Building* (New York: Oxford University Press, 1979), ix.

15. Ibid., 119.

16. Ibid., 120.

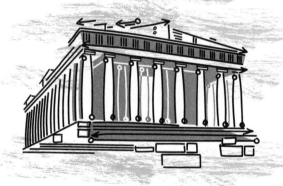

chapter 4

A Pithy History of Architecture

"What's past is prologue."[1]
William Shakespeare

The word *architecture* is a gift from the ancient Greeks who, immediately after minting the term, devised the first penalty clause in the contract with the architectural firm of Ictinus and Callicrates, official architects of the Parthenon. They were also the architects for other rather undistinguished Doric buildings, so it is believed it was really the sculptor Pheidias who elevated the Parthenon to the heights of great art. In any event, the Parthenon has proven that the human race is *not* progressing along any sort of linear path culminating in the present age and beyond. Technologically, there is no doubt about our superiority over our ancestors, but our artistic progress is another matter. Volumes have been written on the Parthenon, each demonstrating rather decisively that the pinnacle of building architecture was reached circa 450 B.C.

Even the demanding Le Corbusier, who never resisted the urge to voice a strong opinion or to gore a sacred cow, said

> There has been nothing like it anywhere or at any period. It happened at a moment when things were at their keenest, when a man, stirred by his noblest thoughts, crystallized them in a plastic work of light and shade. The mouldings of the Parthenon are infallible and implacable. In severity they go far beyond our practice, or man's normal capabilities. Here, the purest witness to the physiology of sensation, and to the mathematical speculation attached to it, is fixed and determined: we are riveted by our senses; we are ravished in our minds; we touch the axis of harmony. No question of religious dogma enters in; no symbolic description, no naturalistic representation; there is nothing but pure forms in precise relationships.
>
> For two thousand years, those who have seen the Parthenon have felt here was a decisive moment in Architecture.[2]

The architecture of the Parthenon tells us a great deal, in our technological time, about sublime user interfaces. What appears to be a thoroughly rectangular temple composed of straight lines with supporting perpendicular columns is actually composed of subtle curves to account for the distortions in human optics. The massive Doric columns bulge in the center so they appear straight, not concave, to the human eye. The columns have an inward inclination of 2⅜ inches toward the top. If this inward axis were prolonged upward on each column, they would finally meet 1½ miles into the sky. The *stylobate*, or base, of the temple gently bulges upward to about 15 inches on the façade ends of the building and 28 inches in the center of the flanks. The radius of this larger curve, if extended into an enormous arc, would create a circle of 3½ miles.

> The general effect of the rising curves upon the platform as a whole may be likened to the result obtained by cutting a rectangle from the surface of a melon.[3]
>
> William Bell Dinsmoor

These are not mere exercises in geometry. They are but two examples of many precisely planned alterations of angles and curves forming the unifying, regulating lines of the Parthenon. Extending axes were a part of the planning. The site plan was considered well beyond that of the acropolis. The axis extends from the sea at Piraeus, through the Parthenon, and on to Mount Pentelicus.

> The whole building is constructed, so to speak, on a subjective rather than an objective basis; it is intended not to be mathematically accurate, but to be adapted to the eye of the

spectator. To the eye a curve is a more pleasing form than a straight line, and the deviations from rigid correctness serve to give a character of purpose, almost of life, to the solid marble construction.[4]

Percy Gardner

Being a true democracy, ancient Greece had a civic impetus to its architecture. It was the people's money being spent, and how those people complained about the cost of this temple to Athena! Pericles, being a shrewd mayor and a wealthy man, said "Fine, I will build the Parthenon with my own money and put *my* name on it." The citizens of Athens immediately capitulated, insisting that Pericles spend as much of the people's money as he needed. And he did just that, providing an enduring object lesson for us all.

Architects have always had to contend with politics and egos, even when they were pampered by royal patrons. Imhotep designed the first pyramid at Saqqara in Egypt, under the auspices of King Zoser, but the design for these structures was often attributed to divine sources while the poor architect did all the work. Justice was done, however, when Imhotep himself was later regarded as a god.

Architects: Anonymous Craftsmen and Superstars

Imhotep appears to have been the first of the superstar architects, although to this day some refuse to believe a mortal man could have designed the pyramids and, instead, give aliens credit for his design. Gods, aliens, or just an architect—we may never know—but architects have ranged from great artists revered through the ages to anonymous craftsmen rising through the ranks.

We do not know the names of the Hindu architects and builders who devised and led the effort to carve complete temple complexes out of solid rock. The shrine of Kailasha began when the builders cut down into sheer rock to isolate a piece 250 × 160 feet. Out of this, they carved intricate friezes, pillars, statues and bas-reliefs. The interior was chiseled out by hand and adorned with thousands intricate figures and animals. A series of chapels and monasteries were then carved into the walls on the three surrounding sides of the quarry encircling the temple. There are many of these temples—Kailasha is just the most highly regarded.

Also difficult to fathom is the impressive Buddhist temple at Bodh-gaya, specifically the fact that it has perfect Gothic arches dating back to the first century A.D. No one in the West can explain this.

The grand architectural legacies briefly described here have not endured in all cultures. Chinese architecture has little predating the sixteenth century because many of the earlier masterpieces were made of wood. And besides, architecture was a minor art in China. Architects were less admired than the great masters of pottery.

> Above all, Chinese architecture suffered from the absence of three institutions present in almost every other great nation of antiquity: an hereditary aristocracy, a powerful priesthood, and a strong and wealthy central government.[5]
>
> Will Durant

The European Middle Ages were dominated by a powerful theocracy and aristocracy. The cathedrals are one result. The architects of these marvels remained anonymous, as did the artists of that epoch, until the Renaissance, when they became celebrities once again. Michelangelo was a celebrity, certainly, as was Palladio, who was the only architect to become a noun—Palladianism. And an adjective: Palladian windows adorn museums, older schools, and homes in suburban subdivisions and look as alive now as they did in Renaissance Venice 400 years ago.

And then there are nameless architect-martyrs such as the unfortunate fellow who had his hands chopped off by a mistress of a French king, thus preventing him from designing a similarly beautiful chateau for her rival.

Modern Architecture: Rise and Demise

Alvin Toffler, in *The Third Wave*, describes history as a series of crashing waves of change. The first wave was a revolution in civilization resulting from man's invention of agriculture about 10,000 years ago. This wave transformed human society from small, nomadic bands foraging and hunting for food to inhabitants of village life and, eventually, modern society. Architecture was born in the first wave as settlements became more sophisticated and structures took on meaning greater than mere shelter from the elements.

The second wave was, and is, the Industrial Revolution. It began in the 1600s, when humans and animals ceased to be the sole sources of energy and production. Machines and fuels changed every aspect of life, from family patterns to communications, politics, business, and economics.

The modern age of architecture, when everything changed aesthetically, began with the second wave. As Jonathan Hale points out in *The Old Way of Seeing*, the word *normal*, which previously meant "right-angled," only took on its modern meaning in 1828. A certain gaiety—a willingness to do something for its own sake—was being lost. Men no longer wore ruffled shirts, plumes, wigs, and colorful tights. Even women now wore somber clothes. Correctness was placed above inspiration on the hierarchy of virtues, and sobriety was more rigidly enforced.

> The key to the period [1820–40] appears to be that the mind had become aware of itself.[6]
>
> Emerson

Architecture, too, became self-conscious and calculating. The intuitive geometries, patterns, and regulating lines used to design the great legacies of the past were replaced with strict functionality. Buildings became self-conscious, and the joyful aliveness and quality without a name usually was lost. "The timeless way" and the "old way of seeing" gave ground to the beginnings of the modern era, where buildings became social statements rather than just beautiful buildings. And the loss was even greater than this.

The proportions known as The Golden Section guided architects and builders from Imhotep to Colonial carpenters. This way of seeing, this innate geometry, was being lost:

> An egg, an apple blossom, a human face, a seashell—all embody Golden Section proportions. The Great Pyramid of Cheops is perhaps its most dramatic architectural expression, but the Parthenon's façade follows it as well, and Chartres Cathedral abounds in Golden Section harmonies. The Golden Section is also called the Divine Proportion, among other superlatives.[7]
>
> The proportion of the Golden Section is: a is to b as b is to c; and a plus b also equals c.[8]
>
> The sugar maple has the same proportions as Audrey Hepburn's face; she may not *look* like a tree, but she *is* like a tree.[9]
>
> Jonathan Hale

The loss of this guiding principle resulted in a certain discordance between people and buildings. Before, the proportions used in architecture were in harmony with human dimensions and were extensions of them. Modern architectural forms became severed from unconscious human harmonies. We no longer felt "at home" in buildings.

The era of "bigness" was emerging, with commerce replacing barter even in rural areas. Buildings were designed to project "Respectability," "Domestic Bliss," and "Strength," not the joyful aliveness and mystery of the ancient proportions.

As the Industrial Revolution rolled on, buildings became more specialized. In fact, entirely new types of buildings were needed: factories to mass-produce garments, widgets, and newspapers; warehouses to store all the goods; the grain elevators of the

A Pithy History of Architecture

midwestern United States; fire stations; train terminals like the D'Orsay in Paris; and office buildings. New building materials and mass production required complex engineering and new construction methods. The possibilities for architecture expanded exponentially, and a demand for bigger and bigger structures swelled. Public safety became an issue, given the revolutionary changes in scope and scale.

The age of professionalism, licensing, certification, and regulation was born and never stopped. Prior to the mid-1800s, there were no schools of architecture, no degree programs, nothing but on-the-job training. Architects were self-proclaimed and usually were masons or carpenters who had a talent and interest in design. The famous architects often began in the arts. The American Institute of Architects was born in the 1850s, and thereafter, schools of architecture were established throughout the industrialized world.

The Architect as Social Philosopher

Twentieth-century architecture focused its efforts on the new frontier: cities. Architects became urban planners and social critics. In the spirit of utopian socialism, it was assumed by many that human nature could be perfected if the architectural conditions were just right. The traditional home was regarded as nostalgic nonsense, and when inhabitants bridled against living like rodents in mass-produced mazes of cement apartment blocks, the architects, including our friend Le Corbusier, essentially said their eyes just needed to adjust.

But people's eyes never did adjust to concrete tenement or cubist life. The glass boxes were derided as human filing cabinets. Norman Mailer trenchantly said they create dead places in the brain and a profound sense of alienation on the part of those who do not know how to penetrate their monolithic coldness. Tom Wolfe wrote *From Bauhaus to Our House*, a brilliant deconstruction of deconstructionism. Many buildings inspired by modernism have been torn down, and others should be. The roof of Frank Lloyd Wright's Johnson Wax Headquarters leaked.

The modernist experiment did not produce the didactic exemplars architects intended for the spiritual and esthetic guidance of people. Rather than being appreciated for their simplification of complexities or applauded for their valiant efforts at social reconstruction or for their inventive building techniques, architects were simply dismissed. No tangible improvement in public taste or appreciation followed from their esthetic reforms. Despite there being many good modern buildings and many architects sensitive to people's needs and wants, disillusionment set in. The absence of a fail-safe design canon meant that the same kinds of buildings continued to be built but were dressed up to make them *seem* less joyless, less unconcerned, less uniform. The shift to postmodernism was underway. . . .[10]

Paul-Alan Johnson

We are now in the tumult of the crash between the second and third waves of civilization. We are moving from a society driven by industrialization and mass production centralized in urban cores to one based on decentralized information and imagination. The inner cities, with just a few exceptions like New York and Chicago, feel dead. The third wave is burgeoning in satellite cities and in home offices. Sometimes it is hard to see clearly in the middle of a transformation, but it is clear that everything is being affected.

No longer is great new art found hanging on gallery walls. Those are often reserved for the narcissistic, nihilistic expressions of the dying elite of the second wave. Popular culture is where design innovation is now found. Movies, TV, Web sites, fashion, and advertising are visually spectacular and astoundingly prolific.

Aesthetic quality has been democratized. As late as the 1980s, it was extremely difficult to find well-designed furniture, clothes, appliances, tiles, or even a great cup of coffee outside upper-crust urban enclaves—beyond the reach of the "ordinary people," so to speak. Now, beautifully designed goods can be found in any mall or Wal-Mart, while the products of the old-school designers are often just plain silly. Truckers in Kansas carry Barnes & Noble bags with portraits of Shakespeare and James Joyce, as they sip their Starbucks lattes.

At this moment of rapid decentralization of quality and information, building architecture has, ironically, retreated into classic forms. Notice the homes chosen as backdrops for movies and commercials. They almost always have that warm, stolid, pre-war look: mullioned windows, fireplaces, heavy trim, brick paths, wood floors, lots of dogs and flowers. These are the ancient, human patterns of architecture. Modernism does not sell. Suburban subdivisions are filled with traditional brick homes with Palladian windows and cozy nooks.

Some scholars say we are at the end of history. We certainly seem to be at the end of true inventiveness in building architecture. It seems more likely that we are in transition—entering the third wave. As one branch of architecture languishes, having exhausted its second wave challenges, another—software architecture—is newly born and preparing to meet the design challenges of the Information Age.

Architecture and the Third Wave

Conclusion

History illuminates the present and tells us there are lessons to be learned from building architecture. All architects need to study history and the mysteries of design, but we should not try to recapitulate the history of building architecture or make postmodern assumptions. Our own ethos will unfold along with our own 'isms and 'ologies. These will be based on third wave realities, not second wave patterns and solutions. Software architecture is just emerging and will be instrumental in successfully instantiating the third wave.

Endnotes

1. William Shakespeare, *The Tempest*, in *Familiar Quotations*, 16th edition, ed. Justin Kaplan (Boston: Little, Brown, & Co., 1992), 224.

2. Le Corbusier, *Toward a New Architecture* (Mineola, N.Y.: Dover Publications, 1986), 219–221.

3. William Bell Dinsmoor, "The Design and Building Techniques of the Parthenon," 1951, *The Parthenon*, ed., Vincent J. Bruno (New York: W.W. Norton & Co., 1974), 184.

4. Percy Gardner, *Grammar of Greek Art* in William Bell Dinsmoor, "The Design and Building Techniques of the Parthenon," 1951, *The Parthenon*, ed., Vincent J. Bruno (New York: W.W. Norton & Co., 1974), 178.

5. Will Durant, *The Story of Civilization: Our Oriental Heritage* (New York: Simon & Schuster, 1954), 741.

6. Ralph Waldo Emerson, in *The Old Way of Seeing*, Jonathan Hale (Boston: Houghton Mifflin Co., 1994), 42.

7. Jonathan Hale, *The Old Way of Seeing* (Boston: Houghton Mifflin Co., 1994), 61.

8. Jonathan Hale, *The Old Way of Seeing* (Boston: Houghton Mifflin Co., 1994), 61.

9. Jonathan Hale, *The Old Way of Seeing* (Boston: Houghton Mifflin Co., 1994), 69.

10. Paul Alan Johnson, *The Theory of Architecture: Concepts, Themes, & Practices* (New York: Van Nostrand Reinhold, 1994), xiv.

Architect   Software Architect
Builder   Software Builder
Scientist   Software Scientist
Engineer   Software Engineer

chapter 5

The Roles of Software Construction

"To make the architect's crucial task even
conceivable, it is necessary to separate the
architecture, the definition of the product
as perceivable by the user, from its implementation."[1]

Frederick P. Brooks, Jr.

Architect, builder, engineer, scientist—these are distinct professions that even kids on Career Day can understand and visualize. The roles of these professionals are woven into the fabric of our lives, and all of us know roughly what to expect of them, what their work products are, what tools they use, how they are held accountable, and how they are trained. We also develop an intuitive sense of where these professionals' talents and aptitudes lie and whether or not we would personally gravitate toward one of these particular roles in life. Indeed, that is the entire point of Career Day.

**Architect,
Builder,
Engineer,
Scientist**

Now take those same words—*architect, builder, engineer, scientist*—and put the word *software* or *computer* before any of them. Suddenly, the clarity of images turns into a dense fog. It is often impossible, or just arbitrary, to differentiate between job titles and working roles of people building software. And that is where our problems begin and where the software industry remains mired. Were you to ask a sampling of CEOs, CIOs, or even software professionals themselves what the concrete differences are between software engineers, architects, programmers, and computer scientists—their tasks, roles, and accountabilities—they could not answer in a consistent way. The answers would be vague, overlapping, and highly divergent, because there is little face validity to the titles or standardization of the roles. What inevitably follows is our lack of predictability of process and outcome.

This lack of role definition, differentiation, and accountability lies at the crucial *radix* of software failure. And the failures will not end until this root cause is fixed. The fix begins with the acceptance of the universal meanings of these words—*architect, builder, engineer, scientist*—and the rejection of the amorphous nature of their current usage in the software industry.

It is the analogy between building and software construction that provides the framework, the cognitive map, the template for clarity of titles and predictability of roles, skills, and construction processes. Only with this clarity will we see the software industry liberated from the crisis in quality, cost, aesthetics, and accountability.

Guiding Principles

Each profession requires a simple organizing theme, or guiding principle, to define itself and shape its mission. For example: Doctors heal, teachers impart knowledge, and chefs prepare food. These foundational guiding principles have been missing in the software industry. We accept software engineers who are sometimes architects, computer scientists who also build, and builders who often engineer, design, or construct—often without a blueprint or model. In other words, in the software industry, our roles are self-styled and our titles not reliably predictive or concordant with our roles, skills, training, and experience.

Software engineers, especially, are now trying to define and establish their true profession, but they and others continue to use the words *scientist, builder, engineer,* and *architect* without underlying guiding principles. As a result, the words have no potency, and the effort to define the profession flails in the fog of confusion. Software engineers have not recognized the power and organizing simplicity of the analogy or fully accepted the meaning of their titles.

But back to Career Day: The guiding principles of these traditional professions—architect, scientist, engineer, and builder—are very clear and might be presented to a class of schoolchildren in the following way:

- The architect says: I decide how the building will look.
- The scientist says: I do research and invent, to further knowledge.
- The engineer says: I make sure the building will be structurally sound.
- The builder says: I construct the building.

It is not up to software architects to define the professions of computer science, software engineering, or programming. We can, however, define our profession and tell other software professionals how we see their roles in our projects and how we plan to utilize their skills. By defining and fulfilling our role as software architects, the clarity will cascade through the ranks of other software professionals via our plans and their implementation. Our clients, and ourselves, will validate this process, as we both will be committed to **architecture-driven software construction** consistent with the analogy.

It is impossible to overstate the fact that the clients and consumers of software construction efforts will be the final arbiters and catalysts for this transformation in our industry. They will be the ones to hire architects committed to this approach, along with software professionals who fulfill their classic roles of engineers, scientists, and builders. Clients and employers will create these positions, and they will be writing the job descriptions. Clients will decide if they want architects to design, engineers to maximize strength and rigor, and programmers to create the building blocks of code. And, to a large degree, they already have.

As architects, we need to begin by explaining the analogy and architecture-driven software construction to clients and by emphatically averring that, contrary to Bass et al., we are, after all, *not* "software engineers." We are software architects.

Software Architects Decide How the Structure Will Look and Act

A software architect designs software-based technology structures and is the superintendent of the design during construction. Software architecture encompasses the look, feel, function, and overall organization of software systems. It also determines how software systems will work with existing software structures. Software architecture involves software structures large and small, as well as software-based products and embedded software elements.

Software architecture refers to the work products of software architects, as well as the practice of software architects. It is *venustas*—the design aspect of a building program. Just as in building architecture, software architecture marries technology and function with human aesthetics and productivity to determine how the structure will look and feel to the inhabitants. Software architecture strives to meet human needs, solve human problems, and enhance human activity via design.

Software Engineers Make the Structure Sound

Engineers of all stripes strive to optimize the strength and vigor of structures, machines, systems, or chemical formulas with mathematical and scientific precision. Their mission is to ensure that buildings stand firmly, bridges can withstand hurricanes, machines can function smoothly under stress, and software can handle the demands placed upon it.

It is the role of the software architect to decide how software should look, function, and be configured. In turn, the software engineer evaluates, quantifies, and proposes ideas to ensure the strength and capacity of the design. How much of a given hardware technology is needed to handle the proposed load? How can response time be optimized, given a set of circumstances? It is questions of this nature that software engineers answer. They design the engineering solutions, as structural engineers design elegant innovations that allow bridges and buildings to stand.

Designing engineering elements and solutions—this is the area where overlap has always existed between architecture and engineering. Engineers frequently design solutions that are beautiful, and architects incorporate engineering elements into a structure's visual design. The George Washington Bridge, as a prime example, originally was designed as a structure covered in granite mined from southern Connecticut, but when the pure steel structure was erected, it was so magnificent, it was left without its cloak of stone.

Le Corbusier commented at length about the doldrums of architectural design in the 20th century and believed the best design work of that time—from cars to grain elevators to bridges—was being accomplished by engineers.

> The Engineer, inspired by the law of Economy and governed by mathematical calculation, puts us in accord with universal law. He achieves harmony.[2]

Structures ranging from the domes of ancient churches to sky-scrapers represent a strong melding and interdependency between architecture and engineering. This nexus between engineering and architecture exists because architecture has always depended upon technology and engineering to realize its designs. But in the Vitruvian triad, engineering is a part of *firmitas*. Architecture is *venustas*. The role and organizing principles of the two are different, and the skills and bodies of knowledge are different, despite the fact that engineering can affect aesthetics and architecture affects engineering.

The field of software engineering has been struggling to define itself, but software engineers lack the organizing concept of the analogy and Vitruvian triad to guide their efforts. This has resulted in what appears to be an identity crisis. They, on the one hand, often wish to be regarded as true engineers who can obtain certification and licensure as such. On the other hand, they are having difficulty differentiating themselves from architects and programmers.

In the book *After the Goldrush: Creating a Profession of Software Engineering*, Steve McConnell asks the right question: "What is software engineering?" but ends with no conclusive answer.

> We need to continue working on several fronts—instituting widespread undergraduate education, licensing professional software engineers, establishing software engineering certification programs, and thoroughly diffusing best practices into the industry. The software engineering field will need at least 10–15 years to create a true profession of software engineering.[3]

McConnell, along with many software engineers, carves out computer scientists as a breed apart but sees the software engineer as everything else: an architect when designing, a programmer when coding, and at times, a true engineer worthy of licensure.

If this is to be the case—if software engineers wish to be defined as fulfilling all these roles, they should dispense with the title "software engineer" and adopt the more fitting label "archigeer," or "engitect." At other times, they get it nearly right. Steve McConnell writes

> The level of engineering prowess determines how large a system can be built successfully, how easy it will be to use, how

fast it will operate, how many errors it will contain, and how well it will cooperate with other systems.[4]

Now, this statement more closely describes the role of the software engineer if the analogy is used as an organizing principle, but it misses the mark in one respect. The software engineer does not determine how easy the system is to use. The architect designs the function and usability design of the system—how it is used—while the engineer could conduct usability testing to measure and validate the architect's design.

The preceding quote shows how easily software engineers go beyond their true mission and believe they are all things to all people—that is when the fog rolls in. Achieving optimum vigor, strength, and reliability is their role, and it is what they are licensed to ensure. There are some professionals who refer to themselves as software engineers who are actually accomplished architects, or both. This is fine, of course, as long as there is an awareness of the different roles and accountabilities involved and that they fulfill each role.

Software engineers are exploring the issue of certification and licensure as a means of gaining professional credibility and standardization. This is, perhaps, an impulse in the right direction, but first they need to differentiate themselves from other professionals and define their role. A merged role of architect-engineer-builder is too unwieldy. Isn't it time to acknowledge that these three roles are too specialized and complex to be merged into one profession? Software architects—or anyone who believes in the analogy—would say software engineers are engineers, and the word and role are clear: Software engineers make the structure sound.

Also, when software engineers refer to themselves as architects, they frequently are alluding to design done at the technical, "in the walls" level, not the true architectural level. The engineering worldview is from the perspective of the technical aspects of a system, and engineers use the term *architecture* to describe the design of what would be analogous to engineering elements and beams, bearing walls, and other structural systems.

Engineers typically do not see from the classical architectural vantage point of the client and the entire enterprise or domain. So, when they use the words *architecture* and *architect* to describe their work, they bring the *gravitas* of the terms but fail to bring the meaning, leaving the real architectural work undone and the classical role unfulfilled. They are looking at the software as engineers and functioning largely as engineers, but persisting in believing that what they do is *architecture*.

As a result of this Herculean mission of trying to be architects-engineers-builders, engineers are biting off more than they can reasonably chew. They are putting too much weight on their shoulders and, consequently, also feel forced to assume too much blame for software failure. In software engineering journals or on software engineering Web sites, it is common to find them exhorting their colleagues to be more disciplined and rigorous in their effort to create more reliable software. Their frustration is evident in statements like, "If only we work harder to learn from our mistakes..." or "We need to systematically employ higher standards. ..."

This is all so dispiriting and demoralizing. In what other field of human endeavor is it necessary for colleagues to wear hair shirts and verbally admonish each other in this way? Certainly, buildings require state-of-the-art engineering to stand, but structural engineers do not have a crisis on their hands. The buildings always work, whether elaborate or simple.

In their search for answers to the alarming rate of software failure, software engineers repeatedly caution against a belief in "silver bullets." They believe that simple answers would not do justice to the complexities of technology. They prefer to create ever more exhaustive reams of end-user requirements and ever more reliable techniques in their tireless, methodical search for project success. All their efforts rest on the premise that flawless engineering will solve the problem.

Alan Cooper, in his book *The Inmates Are Running the Asylum*, eloquently documents the problems with the assumption that engineering alone will solve the crisis in software. An excerpt will have to suffice:

> The high-tech industry has inadvertently put programmers and engineers in charge, so their hard-to-use engineering culture dominates. Despite appearances, business executives are simply not the ones in control of the high-tech industry. It is the engineers who are running the show. In our rush to accept the many benefits of the silicon chip, we have abdicated our responsibilities. *We have let the inmates run the asylum.*

> When the inmates run the asylum, it is hard for them to see clearly the nature of the problems that bedevil them. When you look in the mirror, it is all too easy to single out your best features and overlook the warts. When the creators of software-based products examine their handiwork, they overlook how bad it is. Instead they see its awesome power and flexibility. They see how rich the product is in features and functions. They ignore how excruciatingly difficult it is to use, how many mind-numbing hours it takes to learn, or how it diminishes and degrades the people who must use it in their everyday lives.[5]

There *is* a fundamental problem of engineers not being able to see beyond their own ethos and worldview. Their assumption is persistent: Software construction only needs perfect engineering to stand. Despite the increasing emphasis on an architectural approach and design, software engineers have failed to see that the classical role of the architect and the guiding principles of the analogy are missing and that this omission is the cause of the failures—not bad engineering. We have been trying to build elaborate, complex software structures without the organizing power of the Vitruvian triad. Of course the buildings collapse, list to the side, or just drive the inhabitants to distraction.

Software engineers are absolutely correct in their assessment that more reliable software engineering practices are important. With that mission alone they will have their hands full. And with their profession and role defined and organized around that mission—not on architecture and building—they can achieve exactly that. Software engineers will enable software skyscrapers to stand solidly, but it will be the architects who determine that a structure will look like the Empire State Building. And it will be in the hands of the "developers" to build.

"Developers" Build the Structure

The lyf so short, the craft so long to lerne. . . .[6]

Geoffrey Chaucer

A far better word than *developers* is sorely needed to describe the builders of software structures. To *develop* is to unfold, uncover, and make known. Film develops until the image unfolds through its contact with processing chemicals. Children develop into adults. Houses do not develop and neither does software. It is built. Homes and software do develop over time. Homes get new features, upgraded appliances, different paint colors, even additions and pools. Software can develop in the same way. That, however, does not transform *builders* into *developers*.

A programmer is also a builder, but not all builders are programmers, so the word *programmer* is not suitable to describe software builders. The building trades have many specialties such as plumbers, electricians, masons, carpenters, laborers, cabinetmakers, and painters. In software construction, as well, there are DBAs, testers, Web programmers, and programmers with expertise in various methods of assembly using a variety of unique tools. These titles are precise and reflect the actual work to be done, but it will be up to the "development" profession to clarify its lexica and "develop" a term that describes their branch of the Vitruvian triad, *firmitas* ("fermitechies"?).

If the analogy is accepted, "developers" will need to change their title. In building construction, a developer is the entrepreneur who masterminds real estate developments, like planned residential communities and office parks. The people who actually build are named according to their specific function. Their titles reflect their skills and roles, and this needs to be the case in software.

The confusion found in the "developer"/programmer nomenclature is aided and abetted by human resource departments who use titles as an odd form of compensation. If you deserve more money, they believe, because of merit and/or seniority, you also deserve an overloaded title, even if it bears no relation to your role. There are even movements afoot to assign numerical grades to the programming ranks, with title changes as you climb the rungs. And the title that sits at the top is, yes, *architect*. This is akin to a talented plumber receiving promotions for his or her fine plumbing work until, finally, being promoted to architect.

So the builders of software suffer from the same laxity of lexica found in the other branches of software construction, and they bear the same consequences. Whatever their titles, though, their role is simply to build software according to the architectural plan. They construct with code, the building material of software. "Developers" write and assemble code in conformance with the plan and complete the low-level design—that is, whatever the architect does not specifically detail.

As in building construction, there are software developers with varying specialties and levels of skill, talent, and experience. At one end of the continuum are those who perform routine work under supervision; at the other end are "developers" who are noted artisans and innovators. It's important to remember, though, that while the analogy holds true in terms of the roles, titles, and processes in software and building construction, the historical contexts are completely different and should not influence our thinking as software professionals.

In the building industry, the prestige accorded the building trades has declined in the last century—along with the prestige of architects, in many quarters. There is more mass production of buildings ("McStick" houses, "McMansions," etc.) and less individual artistry and detailing required from the building trades. Building materials have changed, especially in North America, from stone and solid wood to Styrofoam, 2 × 4s, OSB wafer board, and prefab trim. Brick is used as "ceramic paint," and you can poke a finger through the "stucco" walls. Because less talent and skill are demanded from builders, they are afforded less stature.

As an aside, note that while many people bemoan the loss of individual artistry in our buildings, it has enabled people to purchase more home at less cost and permitted those with lower income levels to own their own homes. So, in a sense, the demand for less expensive homes and the lack of demand for artistry and individuality have allowed builders to produce less expensive products. The other side of the argument is that homeowners are not sufficiently exposed to fine architectural options and do not know enough to demand them. These two forces drive each other, as they would in software.

We need to be careful not to impose today's view of builders onto "developers." The role and processes of software construction are analogous to building construction—but the prestige associated with the occupations is distinct. Classically, it was craftsmen—the builders—who constructed the magical, happy towns of old, not urban planners. It was from these ranks that architects emerged. It was builders who possessed the powers of calculation and intuitive geometries that have been lost to the building trades in the last century.

That is not to say that fine craftsmen do not exist anymore. They certainly do, and sometimes they are let down by architects and must compensate for their mistakes. In a post and beam home, as an example, a noted architect completed the design but ignored the electrical wiring problem that exists in timber-framed, post and beam, stress-skin construction. The massive frame of the home is exposed to the interior and enclosed by foam-filled panels, like a shell. The floors are thick tongue-and-groove wood that also forms the ceiling for the floor below. So there are no exterior sub-walls and no subfloors through which to run electrical wires (or plumbing—another story).

The only place to hide wires is through interior walls or to run them visibly across beams and down posts in unsightly wire mold casings. The electrician on the job was a true master and took the problem on as an artisan. Not only were the wires totally invisible, but the circuit box was a work of art, with each wire coming into the box in perfect parallel unison and turned at a precise right angle. There was no question that this electrician was a fine designer of electrical systems.

The software field is replete with "developers" with this level of talent and creativity, and they have done much to craft their own, unique aesthetic. They have built upon the work of Christopher Alexander to bring ancient pattern language to their work (to the surprise, initially, of Mr. Alexander himself). "Developers" have adapted the architectural patterns studied and described by Mr. Alexander (i.e., the bay window pattern, zen view, and half-hidden garden) and brought them to bear on technical software design.

The pattern movement in programming and "development" is intriguing, but it is not architecture. The role of "developers" is to design and build the technical, low-level components and systems. An Alexandrian pattern describes an architectural heuristic that has evolved over time and is ingrained in our minds. In a sense, patterns are wonderful clichés. Familiar to us all are patterns like "staircase well," "sitting circle," "child caves," and "trellised walk."

In building architecture, these patterns are used by the architect in the design of the home. "Developers" have taken patterns and adapted them for use in the technical inner workings of programming code. This would be analogous to plumbers adapting architectural patterns to find new ways to lay pipes. It is a good thing that "developers" want to use low-level patterns, but they should not be referred to as *software architecture* or *architectures*. We have to be careful not to confuse construction patterns with the design patterns used by architects.

Architects and builders have always depended upon each other and provided a positive force for change upon each other's work. Architects challenge the mettle of the builders and expand their cache of skills, while builders, in turn, challenge and expand the design possibilities for architects. Builders have classically been the artists and innovators who have meticulously made solid rock appear fluid and carved entire human sagas into wood.

While there are hybrids that take on the dual role of architect-builder or engineer-builder, the roles typically attract people of differing temperaments and personalities. Without "developers'" unique talent for blending logic, parsimony, inquisitiveness, and inventiveness, software architects would be forced into a design repertoire of McStick software or, at best, McMansions.

Computer Scientists Further Knowledge

The Roles of Software Construction

The role of the computer scientist is to perform research, invent, conduct investigations, and write to further the body of knowledge of computing, both hardware and software. Scientists propose and refine theories and establish fact through experimentation and the exploration of empirical evidence. They further knowledge in this way in academic settings, government, and for private industry engaged in new product research and development. This is what scientists do, and yet in the world of computing, *computer science* has come to mean other things.

Computer science was the first label applied to departments of computing in academia, and it persists as a general rubric for many departments today, even though students and professors are involved with much more than science, per se. "Computer science" was a fitting title in the 60s and 70s, when the body of knowledge was small and everything related to the field involved exploration and science. We were all scientists back then, in this respect.

Now, though, the role and title need to be consistent with the analogy. If words are to mean what they say, it's obvious that science departments should produce scientists, engineering departments engineers, architecture departments architects, and programming departments programmers. The computing field requires this level of specialized skill, and the individual professions will reap the benefits of individual degree programs.

Once "computer science" is truly that, it can fully focus on furthering knowledge. And once engineering, construction, and architecture are defined as distinct bodies of knowledge, computer science will be able to direct its research, tools, and studies in a targeted way.

The Role of the Client

... to thine own self be true . . .[7]

William Shakespeare

The role of the client is *utilitas*, the side of the Vitruvian triad that represents the need or desire for a construction project. The client represents an entire leg of the triangle and plays a vital role during the design and construction phases, and certainly after construction ends. The client and inhabitants will be the ones affected by the results as long as they occupy the structure.

> Software is not just a device with which the user interacts; it is also the generator of a space in which the user lives. Software design is like architecture: When an architect designs a home or an office building, a structure is being specified. More significantly, though, the patterns of life for its inhabitants are being shaped. People are thought of as inhabitants rather than users of buildings.[8]
>
> Terry Winograd

Or, as Winston Churchill said:

We shape our buildings, thereafter they shape us.[9]

The client is an active participant in the design process, collaborating with the architect in an iterative way until the design is refined to a shared vision of the final result. The role of the client is to simply get what they really want and need, insisting upon an understanding of what is going to be built.

The client should resist being intimidated by jargon and lingo spewed like fountains, or by slick charts, buzzwords, or trendy features. The analogy holds; it has been no different in building construction.

> If they read somewhere that large plate glass picture windows were a good idea, they accept this as wisdom from a source wiser than themselves—even though they feel more comfortable sitting in a room with small windowpanes, and say how much they like it. But the fashionable taste of architects is so pervasive that people will believe, against the evidence of their own feelings, that the plate glass window is better. They have lost confidence in their own judgment. They have handed over the right to design, and lost their own pattern languages so utterly that they will do anything architects tell them.[10]
>
> Christopher Alexander

What CTO or CIO could not replace the term *plate glass picture windows* with some technology that they now reject? Or wish they had? The scanners at the IRS are a prime example.

In addition to getting what they really want and need, clients should insist that they be given plans that convey a true understanding of what is going to be built. The client needs to be able to validate the plan, the construction process, and the final result. This is done in a way thoroughly analogous to building construction. The client does not have to know how to build the house, how the tools are used, or what the technical terms mean. But the client is able to validate progress against the plan to see that what is being built conforms to the plan.

Finally, the clients play the most critical role in the transformation of the software industry's moving away from failed projects toward clarity and success. If clients accept the analogy, use it as the powerful, simple tool it is, and insist upon hiring true architects, scientists, engineers, and builders, the software industry will follow. Only in response to client demand will we see degree programs, research, tools, training, publishing, and bodies of knowledge attuned to the separate disciplines. The clients are and will be the driving force behind *architecture-driven software construction*.

After all, software professionals can debate the analogy, claim turf, parse the lexica, and publish screeds of self-referential justifications and ignominious emails. They can do all these things but be rendered mute and irrelevant if they fail to sell their software construction ideas to clients. The software industry needs clients to wield this power, and we believe the analogy gives them the tool. It is not software professionals but rather the millions of individual decisions made by clients and consumers every day in a free market that drive the refinement and lasting value of these ideas.

Nontechnical people—clients, inhabitants, consumers, or just the general public—have fallen prey to the assumption that software can be judged only according to technical, engineering standards: efficient, reliable, faster (and ever mysterious). Christopher Alexander, who was somewhat surprised to find "developers" inspired by his work on architectural patterns, writes of his perceived disadvantage in judging the resulting software:

> Do the people who write these programs, using Alexandrian patterns, or any other methods, *do they do better work*? Are the programs better? Do they get better results, more efficiently, more speedily, more profoundly? Do people feel more alive when using them? Is what is accomplished by these programs, and by the people who run these programs and by the people who are affected by them, better, more elevated, more insightful, better by ordinary spiritual standards?
>
> Here I am at a grave disadvantage. I am not a programmer, and I do not know how to judge programs. . . . [11]

First of all, *elevated*, *spiritual*, and *insightful* are words rarely heard on the lips of lowly "end-users," but we could say to Mr. Alexander and all others who are equally mystified: With the analogy in hand you *can* judge software. You can understand how it is designed, how it is constructed, and how it functions. You can judge the ease with which you navigate its rooms and how those rooms make you feel. Does a kitchen make you feel alive, as though you could cook all day? Can a software room be so enjoyable you lose all track of time and feel the computer is an extension of your mind?

That is the "quality without a name," and it can be experienced by anyone, technical or not, when they inhabit either a building or software structure.

Defining, Not Limiting

Architect, engineer, scientist, and builder: These roles are interdependent, and each exerts an influence on the others. Each is constrained or empowered by the others, and none can advance too far beyond the others. A design cannot be implemented if it is beyond the science, building, or engineering expertise available. Likewise, advanced science, engineering, and building techniques require a design that meets the clients' needs with integrity, unity, and harmony.

For this reason, the acceptance of the analogy by these professions will define but not limit them. Accepting the classical role definitions, predictability of processes, and lexica will free *venustas, utilitas*, and *firmitas* to be true to their essential natures. Like a camera lens coming into focus, members of each profession will see their organizing principles and focus their efforts. Only then will we be free from the fog that saps our achievement. Each profession is needed for our software to stand, and we need to advance as individual professionals before we can advance collectively. When this happens, the crisis in software can end, and the Information Age will fully flower.

This professional precision will allow research, books, tools, and methods to be targeted to a recognized architectural process, lexicon, and set of standards. In turn, the methods, tools, and materials needed by the builders and engineers will be precisely honed for them. We no longer will be borrowing each other's tools, methods, and lexica in an inefficient, imprecise attempt to adapt them to our needs.

It is hard to overemphasize the ramifications of precision. It would be a revelation to many nontechnical people to learn that software professionals often fail to understand that a tool *is* a tool, at all. Tools, like certain programming techniques or languages, often are seen as synonymous with design and style. This would be akin to a builder of a home averring, "We are using the latest air-gun technology as a platform." Or "The home will be built using PVC pipe architectures."

All the while, our clients and inhabitants are bogged down by these technical *firmitas* confusions while not knowing how to ask *venustas* questions.

When clients make a decision to build a home, their minds fill with highly subjective wishes, visions, and desires. Some clients are quite technical and want the latest innovations in window design, electronics, and construction methods. Others sit on their empty lot at sunrise to see how to best position the house to catch the beautiful morning rays of light.

It's a safe bet, however, that few clients rhapsodize over their future septic system—if they think of it at all. For our purposes, though, the septic system is a wonderful illustration of the differentiation between the roles of construction professionals, and it is a truism that all the features so desired by the clients will come to naught if the septic system fails.

An Indelicate, but Trenchant, Illustration of the Roles of Construction

Like software, septic systems can be intimidating to the uninitiated ("Yikes! All our water and waste stays on the lot?"). But before a piece of land is even approved for sale as a residential lot, an engineering firm is contracted to perform a *perk test* and septic plan.

The engineer documents the proposed septic area and certifies the lot as being feasible. Because a backhoe is needed to perform this engineering function, a septic construction company is typically utilized, and they either employ or contract the engineer.

The architect, in turn, needs to consider the septic field before siting or determining the size of the home. If the septic field is certified for only a four-bedroom home, a six-bedroom home cannot be built unless the septic field can be enlarged. Or, if the architect wants the house to be placed where the septic field is proposed, the entire septic field will need to be moved. The engineer returns to evaluate the technology needed to accomplish the architect's plan and to certify the modifications and obtain approval.

The fun can now begin. There are specialized firms dedicated to the building of septic systems. Heavy equipment operators dig the trenches and lower the concrete tank into place. Construction workers lay and connect the pipe in the trenches and make the connections. An electrician installs pumps.

The completed system is inspected and tested by the engineer and certified as built, in conformance with the engineering plan.

Notice that the architect would have just a summary outline of the septic field on the blueprint. The client approves and validates this plan. In turn, the city engineer validates and approves the detailed plan completed by the septic engineer. And the septic construction company executes the septic engineer's plan.

When the home is complete, the client can use the septic system without a conscious thought (hopefully) and just watch the grass grow.

Conclusion

In this example, the architect did not try to engineer the septic system. The engineer did not get involved in the layout or design of the home, even though the engineering results influenced those decisions. When the builders came to construct the system, neither the architect nor the engineer operated the heavy equipment or worked with the pipes. The client, in turn, did not have to know how to construct septic systems in order to validate the progress being made.

These are the roles of construction. Each professional is a distinct specialist with a clear role, yet all are interdependent and understand each other's contributions. Only in this way can the inherent difficulties and vicissitudes of construction be handled. Only in this way can there be a predictable process and result.

Architect, engineer, scientist, builder—even kids on Career Day can understand software construction.

Endnotes

1. Frederick P. Brooks, *The Mythical Man-Month*, Anniversary ed. (Reading, Mass.: Addison-Wesley, 1995), 257.

2. Le Corbusier, *Toward a New Architecture* (Mineola, N.Y.: Dover Publications, 1986), 1.

3. Steve McConnell, *After the Goldrush: Creating a True Profession of Software Engineering* (Redmond, Wash.: Microsoft Press, 1999), 155.

4. Ibid., 59.

5. Alan Cooper, *The Inmates Are Running the Asylum* (Indianapolis, Ind.: SAMS, 1999), 15.

6. Geoffrey Chaucer, *The Parliament of Fowls* [1380–1386], in *Familiar Quotations* 16th edition, ed. Justin Kaplan (Boston: Little, Brown, & Co., 1992), 128.

7. William Shakespeare, *Hamlet*, in *Familiar Quotations*, 16th edition, ed. Justin Kaplan (Boston: LIttle, Brown, & Co., 1992), 194.

8. Terry Winograd, *Bringing Design to Software* (Reading, Mass.: Addison-Wesley, 1996), x̄vii.

9. Winston Churchill, *Time Magazine*, 1960, in *The Theory of Architecture: Concepts, Themes, & Practices*, Paul-Alan Johnson (New York: Van Nostrand Reinhold, 1994), 269.

10. Christopher Alexander, *The Timeless Way of Building* (New York: Oxford University Press, 1979), 233.

11. Christopher Alexander, in *Patterns of Software: Tales from the Software Community*, Richard P. Gabriel (New York: Oxford University Press, 1996), vi.

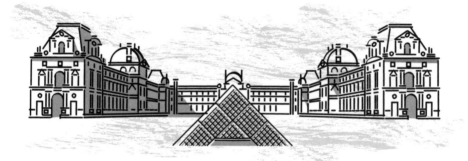

chapter 6

The Role of the Software Architect

"Architecture is an instrument whose central function is to intervene in man's favor."[1]

James M. Fitch

"the most important action is the commissioning of some one mind to be the product's architect, who is responsible for the conceptual integrity of all aspects of the product perceivable by the user."[2]

Frederick P. Brooks, Jr.

While the stature and recognition afforded architects throughout the centuries has varied greatly, their role has unfailingly remained the same, regardless of whether the architect was an anonymous craftsman or a superstar. The role of the architect, as elegantly characterized by the Vitruvian triad of *utilitas, venustas, firmitas*, has held true in the intervening centuries and continues to guide us as we establish the profession of software architecture.

The essence of the role of the architect is design. Architectural design is a creative, sometimes mysterious, process that culminates in a plan for the construction of a structure, be it a building, a machine, a ship, or a software system or product. The design, *venustas*, is what unites the client, *utilitas*, with the finished structure, *firmitas*.

Also central to the role of the architect is communication. The architect is the catalyst whose feet are planted firmly in two worlds: the client's and the builders'. The architect must communicate and enter the world of the client to arrive at the best design and then communicate that design to the builders in sufficient detail via the plan or blueprint.

So, the essence of the role of architect is to design a structure for the client's benefit. It sounds so simple. But how does the architect carry out this role? How does the architect arrive at a fine design? And what is the role of the architect in guiding that design to completion?

The Role of the Architect Begins with the Client

The role of the architect is to design structures to meet clients' needs. To meet those needs—to understand them and fulfill them through design—is both an art and a science learned from years of training and experience. The design process goes far beyond the pedantic exercise of requirements gathering, which tends to assume that clients and users of software systems possess the ability to fully assess their needs, know what the design elements should be, and verbalize them accurately.

If we all knew precisely what our requirements were and how to integrate them into a fine design—in a software system or our dream home—there would be no need for architects; the inhabitants could simply communicate their ideas directly to the builders and have their expectations met in the final structure. As we know, that is how software is now built and why it fails. The very premise of this process is fatally flawed.

The Architect as Client Advocate and Design Champion

There are entire books about software architecture that fail to discuss the client. Some books refer to end-users, stakeholders, and such but ignore the critical relationship that must exist between architect and client. From the inception of architecture as a discipline, the vital role between an independent architect and his or her client has formed a cornerstone of the design and construction process. The architect is, and must be, a client advocate.

Clients can take different forms, such as a committee, especially when public building and software projects are involved. In some organizations and practices, there is a hierarchy of architects—usually associates accountable to a chief architect.

Whatever form the players take, the architect's accountability is to the client, and the architect makes all decisions in that light.

For the preceding sentence to be more than just an ideal or a meaningless mission statement, the architect typically needs to be a professional with a status independent of the builders, especially in complex, expensive projects where conflicts of interest are large in scale. There are exceptional individuals who have been very successful in the dual role of architect/builder, but often, a person in the dual role becomes influenced by profit and cost in design considerations. Corners are cut, and the purity of the architectural design suffers. The "quality without a name" is unmistakable, but it is fragile and dies easily when the design is not the architect's paramount concern.

As an example of the critical role of architect as client advocate and design champion, consider the following incident.

The famous American architect, Robert A. M. Stern, describes porches and verandahs as magical spaces and, like all fine architects, is very exacting on how that magic is achieved. The blueprints for the prototype of his American Dream Home, designed for *Life* magazine in 1994, specified redwood columns painted shell white. The elegant columns were to taper, classically, toward the top. These columns define the veranda, as well as the front entry of the home.

The builder of the prototype home quickly learned that these tapered columns cost about $1,000 each. On the other hand, a straight column could be had for a few hundred dollars. What's the difference? he asked himself, and installed the substitutes. This realized a savings of many thousands of dollars—pure profit.

Fortunately, Robert Stern had the final say on all design decisions. The columns were completely wrong, and he had them pulled out—to the consternation of the builder and carpenters. The proper columns were ordered and the integrity, the magic, of the design was restored.

The current home owners, their teenagers, and their guests now sit on that very same veranda night after sultry Southern night, surrounded by candles, talking until the early hours of morning. They cannot quite articulate why they are so drawn to the space, but it is safe to say they would not think to mention, or notice, the elegant taper of those 12 classic columns. They just know the space feels alive to them.

If Robert Stern, or any architect in the same scenario, had worked for the construction company, the elegant columns would be history, and the cheap ones would stand in their place. The architect would have to accept the decision of the company manager, and that would be that. The owner and inhabitants would lose the magic of those columns, thanks to the inherent conflict of interest between the design, money, and reporting relationships.

True advocacy also depends on an architect with an expansive repertoire, who is able to cull design alternatives from an unfettered spectrum of choice. How can an architect fulfill the role of advocate if tethered to a prescribed set of technologies, tools, or methods, which only narrows the solutions, innovations, and design strategies available to the client?

Individual architectural styles and preferences emerge during an architect's career and are imposed, as it were, upon the client, but these should be the refinements of a discerning mind, not choices enforced by limited skill, education, or experience. A lifelong mason, no matter how talented, cannot necessarily fill the role of an architect. If you use a chisel, everything looks like a rock.

Now, how does an architect—a client advocate—fulfill the central mission of his or her role? That is, how does the architect arrive at the best possible design?

The Art of Listening

Architects spend the lion's share of their time up front: listening to the client and others who will use or inhabit the structure. Listening is an art. We all have encountered people who can talk but not listen, who cannot or will not enter our worldview. Their eyes betray the fact that they are impatient and focused on their own thoughts. They just don't hear us—even though they may be able to parrot our words back to us.

The architect's design cannot meet the client's expectations if the architect cannot hear the client and enter his or her domain. The architect, through listening, comes to know the client's resources and needs, unique challenges, preferences, and the psychological and business climate of the enterprise. The same listening skills are applied to the inhabitants of the structure, and their reality is considered in the plan. By listening, the architect comes to understand what makes the client and the organization tick and how to apply solutions through architecture.

Beyond the enterprise in question, the architect needs to reach an understanding of the entire context and environment. The industry's critical success factors are of vital importance, and the architect listens to understand how the employees and players are motivated and measured—often far afield of the formal performance objectives.

An architectural design that fails to account for the preceeding factors often will work against the client and inhabitants as surely as a home out of sync with the behavior patterns and tastes of its occupants.

Beyond listening, the architect must observe. One architect hired to design software to track and control a large manufacturer's assets actually followed a piece of equipment through its entire life cycle, asking questions of all who came into contact with it. This led to a grasp of the realities that were lying far beyond the words of the client, managers, and employees and their stated requirements.

The Art of Observation

The architect must "design by walking around." It was a critical mistake for the FAA and IBM not to place the software designers in the workstations of the air traffic controllers. If the trained eye of an architect had fallen upon an actual workstation of an air traffic controller, if the architect had walked a mile in the controllers' shoes, it would have been clear that their attention could not be pulled from the radar screen for any significant amount of time. The project managers were concerned that actual observation might have a dampening effect on the imagination of the designers, but in the end, the design was impossible to implement given the inherent characteristics of air traffic control.

The design process begins in the architect's mind from the start and is torn down, built up, and refined as the architect learns more. The design begins to coalesce when all that was learned begins to synthesize and gel. And a vital part of the design involves strategy. The architect asks how the design can be used strategically in the client's and inhabitants' favor. In this respect, a software architect becomes so much more than a person who patches requirements into a software structure. The architect has the potential to transform enterprises, finding opportunities through technology, reorganization, or change.

The Art of Strategy

The ability to see and think at the strategic level is something all architects strive to do. In this way, they can go beyond the narrow view and create software that transforms aspects of the enterprise or create a product with software that transforms the experience of the user. This ability to think laterally can be nurtured but will vary from architect to architect, just as I. M. Pei's talent outshines that of most other architects. That does not mean that a software architect cannot create a perfectly fine software system or software-based product to meet the needs of the client, even without a master's inventiveness and design talent. The analogy holds with building architecture. There are few superstars, but all architects strive to achieve a transcendent design that confers strategic advantage for the client.

So, the role of the architect is to synthesize as much client and enterprise knowledge as possible to spark the listen-observe-design-listen-observe-design cycle that culminates in a design that strategically leverages technology in the client's favor. This is the goal whether the design is for a massive, corporate software system, a software-based appliance, or anything in between. This can be done well only when the architect has done the following:

- Mastered the arts of listening, asking, and observing
- Acquired sufficient knowledge of the client's domain, such as banking, government, education, health care, retail, or racetracks
- Developed a strategic worldview of the client's enterprise, rather than a mere tactical or operational one
- Possessed a wide-ranging knowledge of technology, so a full spectrum of strategic choices can be brought to bear on the architectural plan
- Communicated effectively to the client and builder
- Monitored, inspected, and protected the client's vision and the design

The Pyramid in Paris

Architects are the recipients of accolades for their successful designs but also must take the heat when a design fails to please or is the subject of controversy.

The story of how I. M. Pei (an American citizen, born in China, who mentally designs in Chinese) refurbished the Louvre in Paris (and added a few pyramids) is a study in professional equanimity in the face of severe challenges, as well as a perfect depiction of the complex role of the architect.

The tale begins when the newly elected Socialist, François Mitterrand, decided by presidential fiat to give the Louvre assignment to I. M. Pei as a part of his *grands projets*, a French building spree to realize a new Gallic Renaissance. Socialists were feeling quite grandiose after years of conservative rule, and Mitterrand believed he had a mandate. The Louvre was the first project of its kind not to be put out to bid. The public knew nothing of it—at first.

In a sense, Pei's client was not only Mitterrand but also the French people, French history—even the Louvre itself, a building whose reality had become a pathetic shadow of its reputation. While Parisians considered the Louvre one of their great legacies, only one in three visitors to the museum was French, and only one in ten was Parisian. The visiting tourists found their expectations dashed and spent an average of just an hour and a half in the building—half the average stay at the Metropolitan Museum of Art in New York City.

> When Mitterrand first asked me to do this project I really didn't believe it. It just seemed incredible that he would come to an American to do a project that is as important as any you can find in France. I told the President I considered it a great honor, but I couldn't accept it outright. I asked him if he'd be willing to give me four months, not to think about it—I'd already decided I wanted to do this—but really to see if I could in fact do it.[3]

Pei did not tell his partners of this offer—only his wife, Eileen. He made three secret trips to Paris to study the building and surroundings, walking for hours, ruminating, musing, analyzing, and strategizing. The Louvre had several major problems, as Pei recounts:

> The reason something had to be done to the Louvre is that it was meant for kings to live in, so it never really worked as a museum. . . . you really had to have time to see the Louvre because you got lost in it—you didn't know where anything was and there were no toilets, no restaurants, nothing of that sort.

> When you want to build a museum about 50 percent of exhibit space has to be matched by 50 percent of supporting spaces— reserve conservation laboratories, restaurants, auditorium, lecture halls, public reception areas, toilets, things like that—which it did not have. Tiny little toilets; in fact, I remember very well when I went there frequently, I had to leave the Louvre to find a place to go. And when you leave the Louvre, some people don't come back again. They lost a lot of people.

> The Louvre Museum happened to be a tenant in the Louvre, that's all. It occupied a long, long wing along the Seine—about 800 meters long—and it was almost impossible to go from one end of that wing to the other without going up and down stairs, and therefore most people who went to the Louvre, as I did, probably only saw maybe 25 percent of it. The rest was just missed.[4]

The most frequently asked question by visitors was, "How do we get in?"

Pei studied Parisian landscape design and continued to walk the grounds as the design began to form in his mind.

The Louvre is an enormous U-shaped building with a massive courtyard—the Cour Napoleon. This sacred ground was employed as a gravel parking lot for the Ministry of Finance, another tenant of the Louvre. It became clear to Pei that this courtyard had to be the new center of gravity. It was also evident that the Ministry of Finance would have to vacate the premises, freeing the critical Richelieu Wing.

Pei was not yet thinking pyramids, but he proposed a new entrance in the middle of the courtyard leading to a subterranean entrance hall. Mitterrand was pleased.

The French people were not pleased. As Pei was announced as the chief architect, the reaction was swift. The xenophobic French, already losing cultural ground to McDonalds' Americanization, were upset that an American was selected to alter their national treasure although it helped that Pei had designed a successful addition to the National Gallery in Washington and that he was a "hyphenated American." He said:

> I think being a Chinese-American has not hurt. History, you see, is important to the French and I hope I was able to convince them that I came from a country with a long history and I would not take this problem lightly.[5]

Also, the French still had an overflowing reservoir of good feelings toward Mitterrand, their newly elected champion of *liberte*, *egalite*, and *fraternite*.

Back in Manhattan, Pei and a select group of his associates went to work designing a five-acre limestone subterranean catacomb with an auditorium, storage space, conference rooms, information booths, a luxurious café, a bookstore, and electric carts to transport art.

The new entry would form a hub from which would radiate three halls to the clearly marked wings. The visitor could now reach a wing by walking just 100 feet. A fourth hall would lead to a fashionable shopping area (capitalism: a new wave of Parisian controversy). The new Grand Louvre configuration would have 165 rooms, making it the largest museum in the world. The curators finally would be able to display 70,000 works of art that had been neglected in dim storage areas for many years.

Even before pyramids were revealed, the French were stunned, considering the Cour Napoleon as sacred earth (a parking lot by day, a prostitute cruising area by night). This attitude seemed reflexive rather than reasoned and perhaps an expression of the French tendency to emphatically say "*Non!*" at first, to almost anything.

If French citizens had thought about it, they would have realized that the Louvre had 800 years of architectural history. Each epoch left its mark on the structure. It first was built as a medieval fortress and dungeon and then was torn down to become a Gothic royal residence. In the 1500s, it was transformed into a Renaissance palace, and then two King Louis's commissioned substantial work on the landmark. It was made partially into a museum in 1793 and had massive additions made under the auspices of Napoleon III.

> When Empress Eugenie asked: 'But what style is that? It's not Louis XIV, nor Louis XV, nor Louis XVI!', Charles Garnier, architect of the Opera, is supposed to have replied: 'Madame, the style is Napoleon III. So how can you complain?'[6]
>
> Elizabeth de Farcy and Frederic Morvan

So, historically, the Louvre has never been a static structure and leaders have been unafraid to leave contemporary influences upon it. If they had been afraid, the Louvre would still be a hulking medieval fortress. This historical reality, though, has never deterred the French from protesting changes to their precious edifice.

Pei came to see that the sacred ground simply had to be broken. He said:

> The center of gravity had to be the Cour Napolen. That's where the public had to come. But what do you do when you arrive? Do you enter into an underground space, a kind of subway concourse? No. You need to be welcomed by some kind of great space. So you've got to have something of our period. That space must have volume, it must have light and it must have a surface identification. You have to be able to look at it and say, 'Ah, this is the entrance.[7]

Pei's 70-foot pyramid entry is patterned after the great pyramid at Giza.

> The Pyramide is an extraordinary technical achievement: 70 ft high on a base of some 100 ft square; it is made of 793 glass diamonds and triangles fitted together with pinpoint accuracy and mounted on an aluminum framework supported by 93½ tons of girders and stainless steel joints.[8]
>
> Elizabeth de Farcy and Frederic Morvan

Surrounding the pyramid are a trio of diminutive "pyramidons" and three reflecting pools with fountains. There is an inverted glass pyramid extending underground in the shopping area—the point suspended just above the ground. These structures, as well as elements of staircases, windows, and ceilings, employ the same technological methods and details, all worked out and tested before ground was broken.

Pei believed that no solid addition could ever complement the old Louvre but that the glass structure would reflect it without dominating the scene. And Paris is replete with pyramids and geometric, abstract forms. Indeed, the Place des Pyramides is on the periphery of the Louvre's north side, but Pei maintains that the pyramid shape was chosen purely because it was the correct shape and design, not to mimic other Paris pyramids.

In 1665, the reaction of the French people to Bernini's ornate Italian plan for the renovation of the façade of the Louvre—then the royal palace—forced Louis XIV to send the famous architect packing, even after the foundation was laid. A trio of French architects replaced Bernini and the King turned his attention to the building of Versailles, instead. But Mitterrand publicly promised Pei:

What happened to Bernini will not happen to you.[9]

Pei presented his design to the advisory (only) Commission Supericune des Monuments Historiques on January 23, 1984. Pei recalls:

One after another they got up and denounced the project. My translator was so unnerved that she started to tremble. She was scarcely able to translate for me when I came to defend my ideas.[10]

Pei and his group retreated to the refuge of a bistro and licked their wounds. Fortunately, the Commission had no binding authority, and Mitterrand approved the design without qualification. Pei concluded,

It is a great help to deal with one man only.[11]

But it wasn't that easy. The French recoiled in horror when presented with the design for the pyramid. The Louvre's own curator of paintings compared it to a tacky diamond, and the museum director resigned in disgust; a prominent editorial compared the pyramid's reflective character to the Ewing Building in Dallas. *Tout le Paris* took up the anti-Pei sentiment and wore buttons asking, "*Pourquoi la Pyramide?*" Pei's daughter witnessed women spitting at her father's feet.

Pei remained poised and, of course, prevailed. Mihai Radu, a junior designer on the project, concluded,

> I never got the impression that he was discouraged or depressed. He perceived it as part of his job to make people understand his work. He's a very level person. I've never seen I. M. when he wasn't smiling, and he was smiling even then.[12]

Phase 1, including the design and first construction phases, lasted from 1983–89. Pei explained,

> We wasted two years. It was the media that I had to deal with at that time. I was totally unprepared: My French is just not adequate for that purpose.... It was 18 months of nothing but harassment. People demonstrating and everything. They didn't do anything really serious, like committing suicide. But very close, there were a few. So even though Phase 1 took six years, only four of those years were devoted to architecture and building.[13]

The role of the architect also entails the selection of the right technology and suppliers when they involve important architectural elements. Pei was very clever in this regard:

> The French Government made no secret of it, they wanted everything to be made in France. And the French contractors are incredibly good....On the other hand, the glass problem. You see, the glass had to be clear. It's very thick, it's about three-quarters of an inch thick, and if it is not clear it will be green, very dark green, bottle green. That is not acceptable because the Louvre must be seen and the ochre-colored stone shouldn't look green. So, therefore, I requested a French manufacturer to make this glass. They said: 'No, we no longer make it.' And then finally they said, 'Well, if you build 1000 pyramids, we'll make it for you.' I didn't report this to the President. I went to a German firm and said: 'Can you make it?' 'Yes, we can.' Then the French firm said: 'We'll make it.'[14]

Architects need to know when to be traditional and when to use invention. Invention involves risk and the role of architect includes assessing that risk and deciding how much should be involved in any given project. The architect must also be sure a structure can be adequately maintained. In this respect, even the cleaning methodology for the pyramids roiled into a tempest. But the resolution of this cleaning issue illustrates Pei's practical, problem-solving approach to these obstacles.

> For a long time there was a debate: 'Can you clean the glass?' They would try different ways. They hired some Indian from Canada to clean it. They even tried robots. Eventually we will

clean by robot. But finally, we got somebody to get up there and hang the rope from the tip of the pyramid and wash it. But now one day is all we need, so the washing problem is no longer. But for a while it became quite a problem. Because the French wanted to find any reason to object. Cleaning the pyramid kept us quite involved.[15]

Phase 1 involved the design and construction of the pyramid and the 670,000-square-foot new underground space. Phase 2 consisted of the conversion of the massive Richelieu Wing from the offices for the Ministry of Finance to three floors of new exhibition space—370,000 square feet of it. With this new space, the Louvre became the largest art museum in the world.

A great architectural challenge was the creation of new space within the historic walls, including three interior courtyards used as parking lots. Pei converted the parking lots into sky-lit sculpture courts, and he dealt with some difficult client requirements for the painting collection:

> ...the painting collection is perhaps the most important French painting collection in the world. Not perhaps. Definitely. And yet, people don't go there. The French conservators want it upstairs because of daylight. They are very, very insistent on using daylight. Very insistent. And for that reason they take the attic space. To get up there you have to walk 75 feet, vertical space, and most people don't walk up there. So they miss a lot of visitors. I was told maybe 10 to 15 percent of the people go up to the top floor, and that's a great pity. So I proposed to put in escalators. I hated to do that. It's a 19th-century building and you don't install something like that unless you have a very good reason. That was a big battle but it was won. And today, nobody disagrees that it was absolutely needed. Because, otherwise, the interconnection vertically is very difficult.[16]

Next, Pei demonstrated his transcendent ability to leverage architectural design in the client's favor—including the mordant French public—by solving the age-old museum lighting problem in a singular way. Once again, he employed his characteristic thoroughness in understanding all the factors impacting design, including the culture of French maintenance workers. His extreme inventiveness combined with a practical, problem-solving attitude:

> The lighting of paintings is extremely important—it is never studied enough, it just hasn't been. We don't have good daylight galleries in America.... The skylight is always very bright, and therefore, the brightest is the ceiling. The second brightest is the floor. The walls, where you want the light to be, look dark. And, consequently, we decided this is something we want to do a piece of research on. And I think one of the major breakthroughs, I consider, in this wing, is in the lighting. The lighting solution is this: We make the ceiling into three layers. The

first layer is glass, skylight, with a UV filter, of course, and then below the glass is an egg crate. An egg crate is carefully calculated so that the orientation is such that no direct sunrays will come in. (It would have been better if they were movable because then we would get good light all year around, all seasons. Unfortunately, the French have experience with maintenance crews. They said, 'It won't work here.' And they're right, they're right. So we fixed egg crates that don't have to be touched.) The light is deflected to the walls. It is no longer coming down to the floor. So the walls now are bright, they get light. No reflection, I guarantee that. And that has turned out to be something that the French conservators—they're very conservative—they accepted this. And now they claim it is the best in the world. This they like.[17]

Throughout design and construction, Pei was the champion of both the client and the design. He was confident of his design, and he didn't sacrifice the vision even in response to public humiliations. He had one foot in the world of the client and the other in the world of the builders, the design clutched tightly in his hands. With profound poise, he demonstrated the role of the architect as leader. He said:

> The Richelieu Wing opened in November 1993, exactly 200 years after the founding of the Louvre. The Richelieu Wing, together with the Napoleon Court, is now complete. Therefore the Louvre finally functions the way we had planned. And if you go there now, you will understand why the pyramid was put there. I think the vindication of the whole plan is now made possible through the completion of this wing. You go down three sets of escalators to an intermediate level still below ground and you can enter the three wings of the Louvre. The fourth wing goes to shops, parking, the bus terminal. All the buses that you've seen on Rue de Rivoli, they are all underground now. So, urbanistically, that's another important contribution. At this level, we have the auditorium, we have restaurants, we have a reception area. And we have an enormous bookstore and shops and meeting rooms and a conference center—everything is there. Below this level is all circulation. There is a truck way to connect all the departments underground and there is a large reserve so all the collections—nearly all the collection in the Louvre now comes back home.[18]

This account of opening day epitomizes the final reaction of the French citizens to their new pyramid:

> ...the day that the pyramid was unveiled, curious Parisians came in droves to see it, and they had to admit that the airy structure actually added to the beauty of the refurbished palace surrounding it, offering a focal point in the courtyard and new perspectives through its glass.[19]
>
> Alec Lobrano

Conclusion

After all that—with some critics close to suicide—they loved it. The story illustrates that, regardless of culture, change is resisted to one degree or another even when the status quo is uncomfortable, clumsy, and ineffective. We concede that the idea of a modern glass pyramid was radical, but a confidant I. M. Pei and his brilliant design were vindicated—praised by his former critics. Now few can imagine the Louvre without its glimmering center of gravity.

The story of I. M. Pei and the pyramid is a transcendent one, and his work is a sublime example of the role of the architect and the challenges inherent in the design and construction process. The story yields penetrating object lessons for software architects who can only marvel at Pei's powers of analysis and design as they, themselves, aspire to fulfill their role.

This tale of I. M. Pei begs a question: If the Louvre were a new software system being refurbished without a true architect, what would be the final result? To solve the entry problem, a large square structure could have been built onto a side or back façade of the Louvre. Wouldn't this technically have "met the requirements"? Isn't this akin to the numerous Web "storefronts" created without interfacing elegantly to the enterprises' business systems?

Of course, sometimes a quick Web site is a good tactical solution, especially when time-to-market is the prime motivator. But an architect would be able to make that decision within the larger context of the entire enterprise and design an ultimate, cohesive strategy. Pulling together Web teams who work in isolation outside the larger context leads to fragmented design and is akin to putting a box on the side of the Louvre.

Now, this boxy Louvre entry would have defined an entrance area, kept the elements off visitors as they paid their entry fees, and even could have been designed to match the old ornamentation. It would have been a technically acceptable user interface. Some bathroom kiosks would have met the toilet requirements. A great deal of controversy would have been avoided, as well.

But the lowly "end-users" of the museum would have continued with their disappointing, gloomy visits. Without real architects, no one is held to blame, but there is no glory, either.

Pei shows us that the role of architect includes bringing in all elements and disciplines, such as requirements gathering, site analysis, project planning, engineering, subcontracting, and so on. But the architect goes beyond collecting elements when he or she creates something larger than the sum of the parts. That is true design. That is architecture.

Endnotes

1. James M. Fitch, "The Aesthetics of Function," in *People and Buildings*, ed. Robert Gutman (New York: Basic Books, 1972), 9.

2. Frederick P. Brooks, *The Mythical Man-Month*, Anniversary ed. (Reading, Mass.: Addison-Wesley, 1995), 256.

3. I. M. Pei, in *The Mandarin of Modernism*, Michael T. Cannell (New York: Crown Publishing, 1995).

4. I. M. Pei, quoted from the MIT Technology Day Address. Transcribed by Pei, Cobb, Freed & Partners and published on the Internet at www.algonet.sepw (no copyright).

5. Michael T. Cannell, Ibid.

6. Elisabeth de Farcy and Frederic Morvan, editors, *The Louvre* (New York: Alfred A. Knopf, Inc., 1995), 83.

7. Michael T. Cannell, Ibid.

8. Elisabeth de Farcy, Ibid., 86.

9. Francois Mitterand, quoted in Michael T. Cannell, Ibid.

10. Michael T. Cannell, Ibid.

11. Ibid.

12. Ibid.

13. I. M. Pei, MIT Technology Day Address, Ibid.

14. Ibid.

15. Ibid.

16. Ibid.

17. Ibid.

18. Ibid.

19. Alec Lobrano, *Irreverent Guide to Paris* (Foster City, Calif.: IDG Books Worldwide, Inc., 2000), 99.

chapter 7

The Phases of Architecture-Driven Software Construction

"Order and simplification are the first steps toward the mastery of a subject—the actual enemy is the unknown."[1]

Thomas Mann

"I've got a little list, I've got a little list."[2]

Sir William Schwenck Gilbert

It is noteworthy that the title of this chapter refers to the phases of software *construction*—not the phases of software *architecture*. The point of the process is to build something, not just design it, but the process is *architecture-driven* because it begins with an architect and client and follows according to the architectural plan.

Two Overall Phases

All construction projects can be simply divided into two primary phases: the design—or architecture—phase and the construction phase. This classification can exist, however, on several levels depending on the size and complexity of a project. For example, a large housing development would have a large-scale design of the layout of the roads, subdivisions, utilities, and common amenities, such as tennis courts, pools, parks, and ballparks.

The construction phase would follow to complete the overall site. This would include building the roads, installing utilities, clearing the sites, and possibly building the common amenities.

In turn, each individual home would have its own design and construction phase—often with separate clients, architects, and builders. However, the developer would have planned for each home by defining the legal boundaries of the lots and ensuring that each would be feasible for building. It would also be likely, in most areas, that design guidelines for the individual homes in terms of their size, quality, and style—even their footprint on the lots—would be determined as a part of the overall development plan. In some cities, an architectural review board dictates general design guidelines. Within communities themselves, design guidelines and covenants can get extremely detailed—down to restrictions on the material of flower pots (natural terra cotta only, please). One California community forbids runoff from irrigation systems to trickle onto the sidewalks.

So even before a lot is sold, the design phase for that home can be influenced largely by the context in which it will be built. The outcome will be quite predictable, even to the point where an architect has little to do. Sometimes an owner is given a choice of three model homes—and that, as they say, is that.

This is thoroughly analogous to software-based technology structures. A large bank, for example, may desire a total software redesign. The overall domain and scope—"the campus"—would be defined and outlined before any work began on an individual structure, such as a loan application. The global design issues, such as risk management, are the covenants that each individual application design must heed.

The framework would be the same as for the housing development. The infrastructure would be laid out, the relationships between the individual units would be mapped, the size and number of the individual structures would be planned, and the look and feel, quality, and "covenants" would be detailed—down to flower pots, if desired.

There is endless flexibility here. There is a community in New York made up exclusively of Frank Lloyd Wright homes. Each varies considerably but the desired overall style is the same. There are wonderful neighborhoods everywhere of iconoclastic individual homes that mesh into a perfect whole. On the other hand, there is a planned community in Georgia that forgot to specify the types of fencing homeowners could choose. The result is a chain link—white picket—cedar rail terror.

The point is that each project, whether brick or computer code, has its own design and construction phase. And there are nested layers and meta-levels to design and construct, as dictated by the scope of the individual project. The analogy holds in this case and tells us that when the larger context is not considered, fences make the best neighbors.

Architectural Phases, with Caveats

Architects exist to design, yes, but their eyes remain focused on a point on the horizon far beyond the architectural phases and the completion of the blueprint or model. Client, architect, and builder—all have the same destination in their sights: the successfully completed structure. The only point is to build something and move the people in.

The Design Is Not the Deliverable

Because the software industry has not evolved with the profession of architecture and the clear roles and processes inherent in the building industry, we sometimes lose focus on the horizon. Sometimes we even refer to the design and requirements documents as *deliverables*. Too much time can be wasted in the effort and in trying to cross this finish line, leading to criticism that architecture is too expensive and wastes time.

In building architecture, the client is invested in getting the design right but is most anxious to break ground. The point of the plan is to communicate sufficiently to build, but then we need to proceed quickly to construction. With object-oriented design techniques as an example, the effort in identifying the objects, their attributes, and their behaviors is a part of the design, and from there the implementation can be very efficient.

Finished structures are the deliverables. Everything that comes before is just a phase, a stage, or a milestone. With the analogy in mind, it is easy to expose the misplaced priorities often found in the software industry.

Phases are important, and sometimes construction funding is contingent upon the completion of certain stages such as those of design documents, framing, enclosing, drywall installation, and the certificate of occupancy. This is as it should be in the building and software industries. Progress needs to be measured objectively. But after the owners move in, the blueprints of a house always come to rest in the attic, where they remain—thoroughly

The Phases of Architecture-Driven Software Construction

81

useless—collecting dust and growing mildew until younger generations go rummaging for relics.

With these caveats in mind, and more to follow, the first four architectural phases are presented next. The list of phases is largely patterned after the phases of architecture and construction, outlined and practiced by the American Institute of Architects.

Phase One: Pre-Design Phase

In this initial phase, the architect listens in order to understand the needs and expectations of the client, as well as the scope and scale of the project. The client's key design points, stated requirements, and preferences are assessed. The architect carefully studies the *context* of the project—the entire enterprise of which the project is a part. The needs and culture of the inhabitants—their patterns of activity—come to be understood through listening, observing, reading, and asking questions. The client's resources are determined, including the financial and intellectual capital available, as are the problems the client needs to overcome. The architect begins to strategize—to identify possible solutions available through technology, as well as organizational management and process changes. In short, the architect asks: How can technology, in all its forms, be leveraged in the client's favor? A design direction begins to take shape, with the architect and client collaborating, sketching, talking, and refining their understanding until a shared vision emerges. There is a great deal of give-and-take, back-and-forth. Broad budget and schedule objectives are set.

Phase Two: Domain Analysis Phase

The architect undertakes to understand and document the areas (domains) for which the system will be built and to learn client expectations and needs in as much detail as necessary. The desired behaviors of the system—what it needs to provide the inhabitants—are outlined. The architect assesses the client's business and technology environment and the interplay these factors have with the scope of the project. The domain terms and concepts are accurately defined.

An architect may specialize in a specific domain or call in a domain expert. This is analogous to a building architect who specializes in a certain type of structure, such as hospitals or apartment complexes, or who partners with an expert with this knowledge.

Phase Three: Schematic Design Phase

In this phase, architectural-level designs depicting the domain characteristics and technology structure are prepared. The look and feel of the system—the user interface style—is designed. Prototypes are built, if needed. Lines between phases blur at this point, as architect and client work to get everything right. Migration and risk assessments are performed.

Phase Four: Design Development Phase

Now the architect continues the expansion of detail and design refinement to converge on a final design. All the domain and technology design drawings—that is, what the client needs to validate that the expectations are met—are finalized.

Caution: These Design Phases Are Not Linear

Lists of phases, sequences, and to-do lists are very comforting to the souls of all but the most adventurous of us. "Oh good," we think, "Here's the heart of the matter. Here's the process. Here's what I actually have to do and the order I can follow."

But the design phases explained in this chapter are not linear. They are not even a road map. In fact, the list of design phases exists as much to tell the client what to expect as to direct the activities of the architect. Owners need to know what their active role will be in the design stages; the description of the phases provides a logical, cognitive framework. For the architect and client, these design phases confirm when we are finished more than show us how to proceed.

The preceding statements are true because design is a collaborative, iterative, even mysterious process. It is filled with wayward epiphanies, setbacks, and insights. Ideas come at unpredictable times.

The first thing a client may say to an architect is "I want a flagstone floor on a big patio like we had growing up on the coast of Maine." It would be absurd, of course, for an architect to tell the client to wait for the next phase before delving into this level of detail. Rather, the architect takes this information as grist for the mill, because it says a great deal about the client's expectations and tastes.

The client may, in the same meeting, mention an interesting book on cubist houses, or a fondness of high ceilings. The architect needs to listen and let the client's ideas and preferences flow.

Then the architect can take those ideas and preferences beyond the client's horizon and present design concepts. There is furious sketching going on at this point, representing a feedback loop between client and architect. Some design points will be detailed from the beginning; others will remain vague until the final design is drawn.

Into this coalescing stew is thrown the fact that architecture is technological and often requires invention. Those innovations have to be engineered and prototyped prior to the finalization of the design. This can cause further disappointments, serendipities, and chains of decisions.

As in building architecture, the effort spent on engineering and invention is highly variable. It is likely that the first I. M. Pei pyramid required intensive documentation, engineering, model making, and research. The tenth pyramid took much less.

The point is that invention should be achieved during the design phase and that it needs to be manageable. Despite being four years long, the design phase for the FAA project did not include prototyping the inventions. So how could the people involved in the project even imagine that they had a final design at all? What if the inventions failed to work? What they called a *design* was really just a detailed methodology.

So, in this circular way, with the architect understanding the domain, listening to the client's needs and expectations, completing necessary invention and engineering, and working together with continuous feedback, a shared vision emerges and is agreed upon.

Phase Five: Project Documents Phase

The architect focuses on the needs of those who will actually construct the system. The construction process, roles of team members, and construction sequences are documented. The construction guide, user interface style guide, and test guide are written. The architect specifies tools and methods to be used, as needed. All the details needed by those who will build the system are completed in this phase.

The level of detail documented by the architect is variable depending on the needs of the project and the builders in question. If the architect has a working relationship with a certain builder and knows that builder will be working on the project, the architect can tailor the plan to the builder's needs. The builder may not require as much detail on the high-level, architectural design as others will.

The architect, on the other hand, may need to include highly detailed, low-level design specifications on the documents in certain situations. For example, when a post and beam house is built, a special, modular shell called *stress skin* is used for the exterior walls. This eliminates sub-walls on the exterior of the structure. In this situation, the wires will be visible unless the builders are shown special techniques to conceal them. Consequently, the wiring becomes the architect's province, because exposed wiring would impact the architectural design. In individual situations, it is the architect's responsibility to decide how much documentation is needed and when.

Phase Six: Staffing or Contracting Phase

The architect assists in identifying the actual builders of the system. For outsourced projects, bids are submitted to outside contractors and potential participants evaluated. The architect assists with contract details and in assessing cost. Sequences are arranged and contracts signed.

This marks the end of the strictly architectural phases, but typically the architect remains involved with the project during the following construction phases.

At this point, the focus shifts from venustas, the design phases, to *firmitas*, the building phases, where the structure becomes a reality.

The Building Phases

Phase Seven: Construction Phase

The architect's supervisory role during construction ensures that the original vision is understood and executed. The architect reviews construction-level designs to the degree dictated by the complexity and vicissitudes of the construction process. The architect conducts design reviews and analyzes problems and change requests. He or she also designs the accepted changes, assesses the impact on overall design and cost, and sequences the changes. The architect participates in testing and acceptance reviews to the extent needed or desired by the client.

Phase Eight: Post-Construction Phase

The architect assists the client with the project rollout and the migration to the new system. The architect can be involved with the training of system operators and inhabitants, as needed. The architect assists in warranty issues and ongoing maintenance procedures, as necessary.

Conclusion: The Party Phase

The architect and client meet when construction is all over and reminisce about the trials and triumphs (even the best of construction projects are fraught with difficulty). They hold a big party at a Mexican restaurant, complete with mariachi band, for the builders, employees, and customers involved with the project. Those naysayers who whined incessantly and said it couldn't be done now stand mute, sipping their margaritas.

Endnotes

1. Thomas Mann, *The Magic Mountain*, translated by H. T. Lowe-Porteo, in *Familiar Quotations*, 16th edition, ed. Justin Kaplan (Boston: Little, Brown & Co., 1992), 629.

2. Sir William Schwenck Gilbert, *The Mikado*, in *Familiar Quotations*, 16th edition, ed. Justin Kaplan (Boston: Little, Brown & Co., 1992), 530.

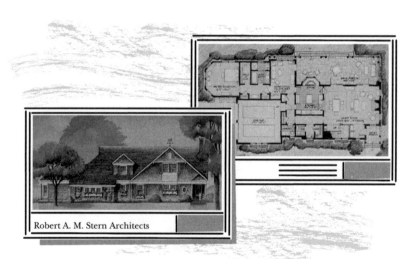

Robert A. M. Stern Architects

chapter 8

The Architectural Plan

"The plan is the generator."[1]

"Without plan there can be neither grandeur of aim and expression, nor rhythm, nor mass, nor coherence. Without plan we have the sensation, so insupportable to man, of shapelessness, of poverty, of disorder, of wilfulness.

A plan calls for the most active imagination. It calls for the most severe discipline also. The plan is what determines everything; it is the decisive moment. A plan is not a pretty thing to be drawn, like a Madonna face; it is an austere abstraction; it is nothing more than an algebrization and a dry-looking thing. The work of the mathematician remains none the less one of the highest activities of the human spirit."[2]

Le Corbusier

The Characteristics of an Architectural Plan

The elemental intention of an architectural plan is to communicate in two directions: to the client and to the builders. The plan lets the client see, understand, and validate what is being built, and, when the structure is a reality, the plan confirms that what was built is consistent with the design. In turn, builders use the plan as their working document. It is the reference that determines their activites.

The plan, model, or blueprint should be able to stand alone and speak for itself. It should not require inference or interpretation to support it, although how to best build elements of the plan can be the subject of interpretation and vary considerably according to the individual builder. But, despite the variations in

89

low-level design, the plan should be able to survive architects and produce the same visible structure in the hands of different builders.

The plan is simple or complex depending on the structure to be built; in any case, it needs to speak clearly to the client and builders. When the structure is complete, the reality precisely mirrors the plan.

In software architecture, the plan is generated from inside out, as surely as it is in building architecture. This means that the overall "outside" parameters of the structure are determined by the interior needs of the client and inhabitants. These include the purpose of the structure; the number, size, and type of rooms; the desired level of sophistication and detail; and the look and feel.

Similarly, the preference or bias toward a certain type of technology (for example, scanners at the IRS) or for a certain method, language, or tool should not determine the plan. The interior needs and expectations of the client and inhabitants need to be the inspiration and impetus—not the imposition of favorite technologies or a design forced by the limited skill set of the architect.

Good Architects, Good Plans

A software architect in title only—who has neither a full cache of skill and knowledge nor a sufficient understanding of the client's worldview—cannot fulfill the role of a true client advocate. Under such circumstances, the client is not being given a broad or correct spectrum of choice and solutions.

In the software industry, this inchoate point often is missed. The design and plan often are assigned to software professionals without regard to design talent or experience. It could be argued that having an inadequate plan is better than having no plan at all, but there are such missed opportunities! An architectural plan can be so much more than an organization of software elements set forth merely to meet the stated requirements.

At the IRS, for example, a skilled architect would have looked at more than the need to efficiently process tax forms, payments, and penalties. An architect could look far beyond the reams of requirements gathered assiduously by all the specialists and consultants. The architect's view would encompass the entire domain—the American tax system and even the entire federal government. Those contexts dictate the behaviors of the IRS: the incentives, disincentives, problems, and solutions. A solid architectural plan addresses these global factors and solves systemic problems.

At the IRS, a skilled architect could have devised a software-based solution to the entire quagmire of the tax code and its bureaucracy by incorporating design changes to that behemoth system. The client could then have decided, with the architect, the feasibility of the proposed plan.

Without this strategic design skill and an architectural plan to accurately drive the construction process, the death spiral of failure begins. Added to this is the constant pressure to "meet dates," which is a healthy impulse when a good plan is in place, but which adds more problems when there is either a poor plan or no architectural plan at all.

Why Have Plans at All?

There are pockets of resistance in the software industry to the very idea of blueprints. This is a shock to nontechnical people but accepted practice in the software industry. Design in these cases is done on-the-fly, and documentation is regarded a necessary evil. Some software professionals speak in highly esoteric terms to justify this stance, saying the design of software must stay in the realm of metaphysics or can be drawn only once the structure is built. Some believe it is more artistic to allow a software structure to reveal itself as work progresses—akin to Eskimo sculptors who whittle ivory, allowing the animal form to emerge organically from the raw material.

Such esoterica is fatuous when software structures are failing all around us. Building architects engage in highly arcane discourses of this nature but always have recognized the distinction between such theories and the practice of designing real buildings. And they have earned the right to theorize, because their work products are so reliable. Building failure is so rare that one such failure is a tourist attraction in Italy—and that campanile in Pisa failed in a charming way.

The Levels of the Plan

The point of embarkation toward a shared body of knowledge regarding software architecture blueprints is the organization of the plan. In this respect, as in all others, the analogy with building architecture points the way.

Prior to the actual drawing of blueprints or the making of models, the architect submits a proposal delineating the goals, objectives, requirements, budget, and schedule of the building project. In software architecture, this is often referred to as the business plan. In either case, this is a written outline of *utilitas*—the client's need for a structure and a description of it in terms of its scale and scope, resources available, and time frames. In software architecture, the proposal typically outlines the *use cases*, which simply describe the primary software actions or behaviors, and also includes major design points and key classes.

Once the client accepts the proposal, the actual plan can be drawn. The entire point of the plan is communication and ensurance that the expectations of the client have been met. The format of the actual plan will vary according to the needs of the project. If two-dimensional drawings are insufficient, a three-dimensional model can be made.

What is called "the plan" actually is a set of drawings or representations that communicates in two directions: to the client and the builders. The plan is layered in regard to detail and complexity. The least detailed representation is on the top; the drawings become more detailed as they progress toward the bottom of the set. Typically, the least detailed, top drawings speak to the client, but are not sufficient to guide the building process. It is, of course, the detailed drawings that speak to the builders.

The top page always represents the entire scope of the project in one glance. This is easy to grasp with the analogy in mind. If the scope of the project is to build an entire planned community with 10 subdivisions and 1,200 homes, the top sheet of the plan would depict a bird's-eye view of the entire development site, with the borders of the 10 subdivisions outlined within the perimeter of the development's property line.

Beneath this overview would likely be 10 pages, each with a bird's-eye view of each of the 10 subdivisions, with the individual building lots demarcated and numbered.

Next would be the engineering drawings showing where the development's utility lines and pipes would be laid, where the storm drains and troughs would be located, and specific plans for road building.

The outdoor designs for common areas, ballparks, pools, wildlife sanctuaries, bike paths, and tennis courts would follow, with separate detail drawings for the building of these areas, such as a cross section indicating the materials used to lay the bike paths, the detailed pool design, and the deck design for viewing platforms into a sanctuary.

Lastly would be plans for the individual homes. These plans would, again, start with a bird's-eye view of the lot with the house sited upon it, followed by a drawing of the front façade and then the back and sides, all showing how the home would be perceived by a person approaching it.

The layout—always critical to the client and inhabitants—follows. The space is composed of primary and secondary places.

A factory, for example, would have the main work areas and then a series of secondary spaces such as lunchrooms, halls, bathrooms, and storerooms. The more detailed drawings would follow, with cross sections and detailed building drawings.

The "spec sheets" follow the drawings. These list the materials to be used; brands of fixtures; standards for electrical and plumbing materials; types of brick, tile, or wood to be used; and any other details important to the architect and needed to complete the building in accordance with the architect's plan. The spec sheets are referenced by number on the main drawings.

The architect determines the design hierarchy with the plan. Whatever the architect draws is to be carefully built in that precise manner. What is not specified on the architectural drawing is left to the builders to design. This level of detail can vary from architect to architect or according to the relationship the architect has with the builders. In some cases, engineers may determine the design of rafters, for example, or a skilled mason may be given the latitude to design an arch and keystone.

Conclusion

The completion of architectural plans, or blueprints, is as vital and elementary to software architects as it is to building architects. The point of the blueprint is communication. It ensures that there is understanding between the architect and the client—that their vision is shared and the design meets the client's expectations.

The plan has one foot in each world. It communicates to the client as well as to the builders, supplying them with enough detail to visualize and build the structure as documented by the plan.

It's so simple and yet not fully understood or accepted by the software industry: Blueprints must be done. The design must be documented, because if you don't know where you are going, any road will get you there.

Endnotes

1. Le Corbusier, *Toward a New Architecture* (Mineola, N.Y.: Dover Publications, 1986), 2.

2. Ibid., 48.

chapter 9

Educating Software Architects

"Education is what you have left over after you have forgotten everything you have learned."[1]

Anonymous

"'Tis education forms the common mind: Just as the twig is bent, the tree's inclin'd."[2]

Alexander Pope

"Software designers should be trained more like architects than like computer scientists. Software designers should be technically very well grounded without being measured by their ability to write production-quality code."[3]

Mitchell Kapor

The challenge of educating software architects exists in a larger, societal context: The clash between the second and third waves of civilization. The uniform, mass education of the young began with the second wave. Prior to the Industrial Revolution, education was a privilege, not an entitlement. Formal schooling was unnecessary for large numbers of people who did not need erudition to supply the sheer human labor needed to fuel an agrarian society.

This drastically changed as machines took over for human labor and people left the farms for urban areas.

Throughout the Second Wave era, work in the factories and offices steadily grew more repetitive, specialized, and

Second Wave Education, Third Wave Needs

time-pressured, and employers wanted workers who were obedient, punctual, and willing to perform rote tasks. The corresponding traits were fostered by the schools and rewarded by the corporation.[4]

Alvin Toffler

Today, many public and private schools remain mired in second wave habits and thinking despite a desire to enter the Information Age. Their large, bureaucratic structures and curricula are ironclad and resistant to the changes needed to prepare third wave students. Individual teachers are prevented from allowing their excellence and individual offerings to shine through by the drive toward regimentation.

When schools do institute progressive changes, they often are in the wrong direction, de-emphasizing critical basic skills in the three R's. Technology instruction often is in the hands of a librarian or media center coordinator who knows far less than many of the students who go home, sign on to the Internet, and communicate to numerous friends simultaneously via instant messages.

Students are rewarded as much, or more, for compliance and attention to clerical detail as for true mastery. Adherence to process drives grades as much as a student's native intelligence, problem-solving abilities, and inventiveness. Rules and order are important, yes, but the emphasis has become skewed. It is now possible for average, compliant students to get A's while very bright, bored students get C's and then run home and get online. Awareness is dawning that many of our leaders were "B students," or even dropouts from college. A saying is making the rounds: A's drool, B's rule. Ted Turner recently opened a speech at Harvard scolding that institution for refusing him admission many years ago.

Many fields always will demand and need students who revere the right answer and are risk-adverse. We want our accountants and physicians to have the right answers, all the time, and we certainly do not reward them for taking risks. But the Information Age increasingly demands lateral, original thinkers who are notoriously noncompliant. Some refusing to fly with the flock are referred to as "wild ducks." Our public schools, especially, are not only failing to foster and quantify such thinkers but are demotivating them.

Colleges are not able to adjust quickly enough to the needs of the software industry, which undergoes constant and rapid change. Despite the rise of software architecture, there are no degree programs for software architects. Software architects must pull knowledge from software engineering, computer science, and programming literature, for example, and adapt that knowledge to software architecture. Books and tools are oriented toward the construction of software, with few specifically geared toward architecture and design.

There is a larger problem than the one just discussed. Software architects typically have a background in computer science or software engineering and then evolve into architects. However, enrollments in computer science and software engineering programs are static, while demand for these graduates steadily increases. There just aren't enough students occupying the desks. In many locales, half the employment positions in information technology are unfilled. Students are interested in computers, yes, and they certainly want to pursue the high salaries in information technology, but they complain that computer science or engineering just aren't their cup of tea. This is especially true for women.

Instead, students are drawn to subjects with more cachet, like marine biology or psychology. A surprising number believe they can take a few courses in computer science or software engineering and still be marketable somewhere in the lucrative realm of information technology. Because there is little differentiation in their minds among the various IT professionals, they do not see the need to master a specialty or large body of technical knowledge. They figure they can get a job with their basic computer literacy and a smattering of courses. When they hit the streets, however, they are unable to find a niche in IT, finding their technical skills just too thin to be of much practical use.

Others enroll in graduate management of technology programs. This places them on a career path toward project management and CIO positions. These students, too, want to be in the technology sector while staying in a "safe place," away from engineering and computer science which is, frankly, scary to them.

All these students are prime candidates for the profession of software architecture. They gravitate toward technology and software but do not see themselves as scientists or engineers.

Still Another Crisis

Vocational choice is a quirky amalgam of aptitude, interest, temperament, and expectation. Some of us were more crystallized than others in our choices, but just think back to how you came to choose your given field. We sort of gravitated toward it based on impressions, experiences, people we had met, and what we felt comfortable doing.

Some 50-year-olds still ask themselves what they want to be when they grow up, but essentially, students cast their future selves

We Are What We Do

in a certain image. They see themselves in a particular role—maybe strolling down Wall Street with a briefcase or teaching a classroom of first graders. Unfortunately, the profile of a computer scientist simply does not feel right to enough students. Dilbert, the cartoon character, has been no help at all, but there is an element of truth in Dilbert.

What Is the Profile of a Computer Scientist?

Computer scientists, programmers, and software engineers tend to enjoy working with detailed information, rather than people or things. They are logical thinkers and tend to do well in math. They are logical problem-solvers by nature, driven more by achievement and mastery than a need for social approval or affiliation. They generally are perceived similarly to engineers.

Certainly, students who cluster around this profile are among those who become interested in computer science. Trying to lure other students with salary data, scholarships, mentors, and the like will not overcome a mismatch of interests, aptitudes, and temperaments—nor should it. Students who enjoy business, social work, or the arts will not be suited to computer science despite valiant recruitment efforts.

Structural change is needed to capture those students who take a few courses in computer science or software engineering and want to work somehow in information technology but choose other majors. Colleges and universities need to create degree programs that reflect the clear roles beginning to emerge in IT, including software architecture. Students should not have to learn to be "builders" or "scientists"—computer scientists, software engineers, and programmers—when they are not interested in construction.

The analogy continues to hold very true. In the building industry, there are specialized educational programs for architects, engineers, builders, project managers, the skilled trades, real estate agents, and even building scientists who study building materials and methods in great depth. If separate degree programs existed for architects, engineers, programmers, and computer scientists, students could gravitate to the specialization that suited their particular constellation of interests, temperaments, and aptitudes.

Architects traditionally have an interest in design. They study engineering and building science to the degree needed to design feasible structures, but their worldview, their perspective, is from the ground occupied by architecture and design. That is what they are, first and foremost. Imagine the absurdity of having the degree programs "Building Science" and "Structural Engineering" and expecting skilled architects to emerge of their own accord following graduation—and yet this what we do in the software industry.

Software engineers and programmers—the *builders*, in other words—see design work as a phase that they are qualified to perform. And why not? There are no degree programs for software architects, and anyone can call himself or herself an architect. They often fail, however, and are pulled inexorably back to their engineering and programming roots. That is their profile, their skill, and their worldview.

Architects tend to have less of a scientific, mathematical temperament and more of an inclination toward design, communications, business, and the application of technology. Degree programs in software architecture would attract a new type of student to the field of information technology, students now lost due to a misfit with computer science and software engineering.

Architecture Education

Widespread formal education and the professionalization of occupations are fairly recent phenomena. Licensed architects did not design the chateaux and cathedrals, nor did engineers certify their plans. In fact, there were no formal schools of architecture until the late 1800s.

> Throughout the nineteenth century, thousands of men and eventually some women called themselves architects and practiced their craft at whatever level they chose. . . . All but a few practitioners . . . acquired their training in apprenticeships, the length and content of which varied on an individual basis.[5]
>
> Dana Cuff

The more formal profession of building architecture was established, of necessity, in response to the transformation from the first to the second wave. The changes of scope and scale of buildings required a standardized, shared body of knowledge. Suddenly, not just larger buildings were needed but also different kinds: customized factories, the early skyscrapers, apartment buildings, train stations, department stores, and office buildings—all with edifices reflecting the nature of the establishments.

Safety became a civic concern, and the professions of architecture and engineering met the challenge through university programs and professional practices that allowed architects and engineers to continue to master their skills through an associate/partnership structure—like that of law firms. In architecture, the university programs largely were patterned after the model established by the Ecole des Beaux Arts in Paris, where several notable architects studied their own countries' educational systems and influenced them upon their return home.

Degree programs in architecture quickly proliferated, driven by client demand. The study of architecture was interdisciplinary, with courses in construction and engineering, drafting, drawing, history, and above all, architectural design. After the rise of Modernism, architects saw themselves as agents of social change, and the social sciences figured prominently in the curricula. The emphasis on social science actually began to eclipse the role of design—tragically—after socialistic ideas took hold in academia.

Software architects emerged in the same grassroots way—through self-styled courses and apprenticeships arising from the software construction trades. Universities and colleges do not yet have degree programs in software architecture, and are experiencing difficulty adding this new focus to a curriculum that reflects the increasing interest in design and architecture taking place in both the private and public sectors. Academia is lagging far behind "the real world" in this respect. It is the employers—the *clients*—who have added the title "software architect" to their organizational charts and driven the rise of this profession. These clients have been defining the role and responsibilities of software architects—not academia.

Rather than responding to this trend, colleges and universities are teaching software professionals to be "builders." Computing curricula is an admixture of science, programming, hardware, and software engineering. But even these areas can be imprecise. For example, software engineering should not be confused with traditional engineering. It is not an engineering profession, per se. The engineers are not licensed. They are not held to blame if software structures fail or have "structural defects," so to speak. Software engineers are not a part of the traditional engineering ethos and do not typically differentiate their role in a predictable way from the roles of programmers, project managers, or architects. They may do all these jobs, sometimes simultaneously.

Institutions educating software professionals suffer as much from the lack of clarity and role distinction as does the software industry in general. Could it be said these institutions foster the lack of clarity—even create it—by continuing to train students in this paradigm?

It will be up to existing software architects to promote and develop a curriculum of software architecture, because current professors in computer science and software engineering do not have the expertise or experience to do so. Alliances may form between business schools and schools of architecture. Do not assume that software architecture would be taught in computer science or software engineering departments. The mental set of computer scientists makes it hard for them to "see" the new paradigm or accept the analogy. They continue to believe that software engineers and programmers create the "architectures."

The critical questions will be the same ones asked by building architecture schools: What courses should comprise the curriculum? How is the body of knowledge of architecture defined? And, how can design—a talent—be taught?

Establishing Software Architecture Education

The formal curricula of software architecture education will be established as the profession is defined and its body of knowledge outlined. But the age-old process of teaching design will present itself. Design is both a talent and a skill. Architects will always vary in the degree of their talent, as do practitioners of any profession. Design excellence is a lifelong endeavor, but the discipline begins in school. Architectural design essentially is elegant problem-solving, and each client will call for novel solutions given the constraints and resources of his or her individual enterprise.

Traditionally, design has been taught by doing, not by studying or through lectures. The Beaux-Arts Institute of Design established *atelier*, or studio, methods that have endured and been used as a basis for all architectural design instruction. For example, the *esquisse* is an intensive, nine-hour session *en loge*, where architecture students, working alone, are required to design a solution to a particular problem. The atmosphere is competitive, with designs measured against one another. The architect Joseph Esherick gives a compelling account of design education under this technique:

Can Design Be Taught?

> About a week before a program was to be issued the title alone {such as: "A Building to Enshrine the Chalice of Antioch" or "A Ski Club"} would be announced, and we could then spend as much time as we could in the library in search of any information related to the subject at hand. This usually meant looking up examples of buildings of a particular type that had actually been built or were projected.[6]

This would be similar to acquiring domain knowledge prior to the design of a particular software solution. The actual problem to be solved, and the conditions—such as a description of the site, resources available, and client requirements—were presented at the beginning of the nine-hour session.

> A major problem to be solved early on was that of finding out precisely what *kind* of problem you were working on—that is, a plan problem, a circulation problem, a site plan problem, or an interior problem.... Initially we worried simply about what the writer of the program had in mind, but later on, to a large extent because the system was so competitive, we had to try to guess not only what the writer had in mind but how the jury looking at our work would interpret what the writer had in mind.[7]

After this preliminary analysis of the problem, the students would begin to draw several small sketches of possible structures that solved the problems and met the conditions. These sketches would be honed to a few workable sketches, and finally, to just one. The final sketch would be drawn in ink and turned in to the instructor. The student was stuck with this design for the next four or five weeks, developing and defending it to the independent jury.

The esquisse simulates real-life pressures and constraints in the shelter of the design studio and forces mental discipline:

> ...in working on a problem on which one is tied down to an esquisse is as strong and as persistent a corrective as there can be against vague and loose thinking.[8]
>
> John Harbeson

Cret comments:

> In trying to improve a poor scheme, the pupil makes a greater effort than he would if you gave him from the beginning the right solution.... {If pupils were permitted to work} together and not obliged to keep their preliminary sketches, {they would} arrive after a time all to have the same scheme, which is either that of the most brilliant student among them, or the one that the instructor has pointed out as the best solution.[9]

Intensive design sessions in the studio—*charrettes*—preceding project deadlines are a part of architecture school culture. It is a competitive atmosphere since the student designs are judged against each other, but charrettes, some lasting days, also are bonding experiences. The student-architects help each other and get immediate feedback regarding their skills. It becomes clear to each of them that design is more than knowledge. Talent, judgment, and commitment are native to the individual and endowed in varying degrees. In the studio setting, students develop a sense of their strengths and weaknesses and how far they have to go—lessons that cannot be learned in a classroom.

Conclusion

Software architects—the designers—have a vocational profile of interests, aptitudes, and temperaments different from that of the builders. Clients and employers have seen the difference and the need for architects, driving the grassroots movement toward a profession of software architecture. These clients have created the positions and outlined the role. Degree programs now are needed to train software architects and create a discrete discipline. Software architects can look to the field of building architecture for models on how to teach the rigors of good design, involving both talent and skill. In school, architects learn what it takes to become a good architect. Following school, they realize they have a lifetime of learning ahead.

Endnotes

1. Anonymous, in *Familiar Quotations*, 16th edition, ed. Justin Kaplan (Boston: Little, Brown & Co., 1992), 783.

2. Alexander Pope, *Moral Essays* (1731–1735), in *Familiar Quotations*, 16th edition, ed. Justin Kaplan (Boston: Little, Brown & Co., 1992), 300.

3. Mitchell Kapor. "A Software Design Manifesto," *Bringing Design to Software*, ed. Terry Winograd (Reading, Mass.: ACM Press/ Addison-Wesley, 1996), 9.

4. Alvin Toffler, *The Third Wave* (New York: Bantam Books, 1981), 384.

5. Dana Cuff, *Architecture: The Story of Practice* (Cambridge, Mass.: The MIT Press, 1995), 26.

6. Joseph Esherick, "Architectural Education in the Thirties and Seventies: A Personal View," in *The Architect*, ed. Spiro Kostoff (New York: Oxford University Press, 1977), 258.

7. Ibid., 259.

8. John Harbeson, in Joseph Esherick, Ibid., 259.

9. Paul Phillippe Cret, in Joseph Esherick, Ibid., 260.

chapter 10

Venturing to Call Ourselves Architects

"Customary actions, as they evolve,
weave webs of meaning among a group
of participants; these form the
very basis of culture."[1]

Dana Cuff

It all began on a wintry day in New York City in 1857, a time of epic uncertainty and possibility set in motion at the dawn of the Industrial Age. Thirteen powerful men—friends of presidents, capitalists, intellectuals, and architects—emerged from horse-drawn carriages to gather together with a singular purpose: to elevate the practice of architecture to a profession in its own right. Up until that time, anyone could hang out a shingle as an architect—and did.

It is likely that those men had many of the same concerns and questions we have today, more than 140 years later, as we begin to establish the profession of software architecture. What is a professional architect? How is one best trained? What is their body of knowledge? How do we go about answering these questions?

Society 140 years ago was in the midst of transformation. Money, not land, was the new form of power, and it was concentrated in the hands of a new class of capitalists. People began experiencing dizzying changes in the pace of progress; by the 1920s, newspaper and magazine articles appeared addressing the problems of stress and modern life—the paradox of the virtues and vices of affluence. Even the scale of the physical world changed as skyscrapers were erected. Architecture rose as a profession to meet those demands.

We, too, are in transformation. Information technology is revealing itself as a new currency, with new wealth concentrated in the hands of a new class of entrepreneur. We might now consider the people of the Industrial Age as quaint, yet we are in the throes of a similar pace of change, except that our new skyscrapers are not creating urban canyons. Our skyscrapers are largely invisible information structures and networks, burgeoning into behemoths.

The profession of building architecture was established to meet the demands of the Industrial Revolution. The scope and function of buildings increased dramatically in both quality and quantity, while the need arose for a formal profession to design new kinds of buildings and ensure that standards were met, keeping those buildings sound and safe. The same can be said of software-based information technology structures, and for many of the same reasons, it is time for software architecture to become a formal profession.

What Is a Profession?

A profession is a specific vocation, or calling, requiring knowledge in a defined branch of learning. *Profession* also refers to the collective body of people engaged in the practice of that vocation. They have established methods of training and education, professional standards, a predictable role, and similar work products and processes, and they have acknowledged mastery over a defined body of knowledge.

Currently, the term *software architecture* is used imprecisely, with software architects having varying roles, skills, knowledge, and experience. Software architects now must cull their knowledge from other disciplines and create an amalgam of know-how. In practice, it is clear that software architecture is not yet a formal profession, and it is up to software architects and their clients to become the driving force behind the elevation of this profession. A critical mass of support and activity are needed to impel colleges and universities to begin degree programs.

Software architects are designers faced with the need to design their own profession. This begins, as all architectural projects have, with *utilitas*: What is the need? What do we need to define and design before calling ourselves a *profession*?

Client Expectations

In our free-market economy, driven by customer demand, it is only natural that clients, or employers, began the movement toward software architecture. The analogy makes intuitive sense to them, and the concept of an architect designing a structure before it is built and then superintending all design decisions made immediate sense and was backed by clients' financial investment in architects.

Clients devised job descriptions for these positions and decided who was best qualified to fill them. Those hired decided, too, that they now were architects. This development, unaided by schooling or dogma, is profound. Companies large, small, and in many industries are committed to software architecture: IBM, Starbucks, Sapient, Avon, and Siemens, to name a few. And Bill Gates recently was promoted to (or declared himself to be) Microsoft's Chief Software Architect.

Despite this phenomenon, there is too much variation to call software architecture an established profession. When clients hire a software architect, they need to know what to expect generally in terms of the software architect's role, skill set, process, work product, and level of competency. Without a commonly understood level of professionalism, each architect must reset the expectations of each client. A profession cannot have clients saying, "The architect who was here last week saw this job as less [or more, or different] than what you describe."

Software architects acquire their title and role after working in software engineering, programming, systems programming, project management—well, in many different places. Their background can do much to determine their design decisions and perspective. Highly technical people often are more oriented toward the technical architecture and focus less on global, domain, and client issues. But that is not always the case, and that is the point: There needs to be predictability in terms of what the client can expect from an architect.

As a case in point, there is a technical school now offering a master's degree in information technology. The school does not require any prior computer experience. The degree program is generally appealing to college graduates who have learned the hard way that their degrees are not as useful as they had hoped and now are interested in careers in technology. They are given a smattering of courses on how to use common applications, as well as some networking know-how.

The local director of this program was asked what jobs the graduates obtained. He said they were LAN administrators, programmers, help desk coordinators, testers, and so on. Asked if the graduates could perform the role of *software architects*, he said, "Certainly. They could do that."

The client needs to know that a software architect is a true architect capable of designing high-quality software-based technology. All software architects do not need to use the same methodologies any more than all building architects do, and like building architects, software architects have various specialties. But the architectural role, processes, and product need to be predictable to the clients. This will become reality as the profession of software architecture is elevated to include a standardized role and as degree programs in software architecture are established.

Unfortunately, client expectations of software development results have been so dashed that many clients now take a short-term approach, in which small software applications are built one at a time and added to in a modular fashion. With the analogy in mind, it is clear that this is the same as building a bathroom and kitchen on a vacant lot and dealing with the rest of the house later. Yes, we can say that the rooms are functional, but anyone can see the problems and limitations inherent in such an approach.

Only when clients know they can expect professional, competent, large-scale design from software architects, followed by a logical, manageable, verifiable construction process, will this short-term approach end.

A Standard Body of Knowledge

The practice of software architecture is the expression of the software architect's knowledge. For this reason, we cannot have predictable outcomes and consistent client expectations until we develop a standard body of shared knowledge. Right now, this is limited but growing. Clients are driving the demand for software architects, and these software architects are building a knowledge base, brick by brick, project by project.

The knowledge base is accumulating through the millions of decisions made by clients and architects every day. It is passed on through practice, training, theory, research, discussion, and writing, as is true in any other field. We need a knowledge base filled with case studies, designs, theory, lexica, technology, practices, tools, techniques, and communication.

This shared body of knowledge then will be contained within an infrastructure formed by a true profession. The infrastructure, in turn, needs to rest on commonly accepted assumptions. It needs to be accepted, for example, that software architecture is *architecture*, not software engineering or computer science. The analogy is key. If it is not accepted, that is, if software architecture continues to be regarded as a branch of construction, the profession of software architecture cannot be established.

Without the analogy, software professionals will continue to debate semantics, such as the meaning of the word *style* versus *pattern*. These discussions would be completely meaningless if the analogy was accepted and a body of architectural knowledge established. Imagine a group of building architects arguing over whether to call Victorian a *style* or a *pattern*, while buildings everywhere are falling, listing to one side, or being scrapped altogether. Building architects do not *need* to argue over these meanings, because Victorian *style*, Victorian *patterns*, Victorian *elements*, or Victorian *paradigm*—whatever you want to label it—speaks for itself in a solid, predictable, finished, physical manifestation. Labels just don't matter when professionals share a consistent body of practical knowledge, process, and outcome. The works of architecture speak for themselves.

Education

It is, of course, difficult to design degree programs in software architecture before the profession is fully defined and a body of knowledge outlined, but we have enough to start. There is sufficient experience, with a large number of software architects and their clients, to start defining the skills and experience needed to be a software architect. And we can expect that an enterprising college or university will see the opportunity to devise a beginning curriculum and seize the day. This is how things proceed in the decentralized third wave. Do not expect a group of 13 men and women to convene in New York City and make this happen, although that too could yield interesting results.

It seems fairly evident that the curriculum would be drawn from business, computer science, engineering, communications, and most of all, design. Architects need to be trained differently than software engineers, programmers, or computer scientists, and forcing students through programs of study for those professions does not produce architects. Building architects do not become builders or engineers before they become architects, despite the extreme complexity of those professions. While building architects are familiar with related disciplines, their role is to design, coordinate the disciplines, and supervise—not to build.

Current practitioners of software architecture need to assist colleges and universities to establish curricula, because there is no precedence. The profession has been missing, and the vacuum needs to be filled. Current professors have not been architects and often are invested in their own paradigm. Even if they do accept the premise of architecture-driven software construction, it is exceedingly difficult for them to expand into architecture when faced with the daily demands of their current curricula and students.

Once educational programs exist, the body of knowledge will expand not only as a result of the work of new graduates but also from educational research and publishing geared specifically to software architecture.

Identity

A means of identity needs to be established, that is, a way for architects to be acknowledged as architects. Human nature craves order and certainty, so it frequently is suggested that a certification procedure of some kind be installed to print imprimaturs on the foreheads of true architects. This temptation must be resisted strenuously, for some very basic reasons.

First of all, identity is more important than certification at this embryonic stage. And how is one identified as an architect—or a doctor or CPA, for that matter? Identity becomes possible when it can be established that the person has mastery over a shared body of knowledge and accepts the standards of the profession. Since these two areas are not clearly defined and developed at this point, it is impossible to identify a person as having this mastery or acceptance of standards.

Secondly, who would the gatekeepers be? Who are these few people who would decide how the profession is defined and who is entitled to join? How would their authority be established, and why should anyone accept it?

The question of identity—who is an architect?—will be answered only as the profession becomes formalized. Like all good architecture, the profession needs to be designed from inside out, not from an artificial order imposed from outside in. The millions of individual decisions made each day in a free marketplace are an infinitely finer means of definition and refinement than the proclamations of a committee.

Now, it is clients who provide the primary means of identity, by understanding how software is designed and built and by identifying and hiring whomever they believe are architects. Clients have accepted the role of the architect and want it. Corporate departments of architecture, as well as independent practices, are appearing all over the world. The profession of software architecture is truly a democratic movement, and its definition and means of identity need to be true to the spirit of that movement.

A professional code of ethics and standards is more profound than just taking an oath; such a code has to do with living up to one's professional title and building trust between software architects, clients, and other professionals. Codes of ethics are built into all professions from the American Medical Association to the Belgium Sheepdog Club. The code represents an affirmative proclamation of ideals and morals—an affirmation of professionalism. The code is typically rather simple, but it reassures clients and coworkers that the practitioner they are dealing with is accountable to a professional organization and its standards. If unethical conduct is committed, there often is recourse through an established grievance procedure.

Codes of ethics are enduring because of their moral lucidity. The Hippocratic oath is essentially unchanged after 2,000 years. The American Institute of Architects has three tiers of statements in their code: canons, which are broad principles of conduct; ethical standards, which are more specific codes of behavior; and rules of conduct, which are mandatory behaviors. Violation of a rule of conduct is grounds for disciplinary action by the AIA National Ethics Council.

A code of ethics for software architects will become realized as the profession becomes better defined and expectations set, but the process can begin now. All software architects, however they came to be architects, can aspire to fulfilling the classical role and adhere to the belief that they are client advocates with the ability to solve problems and leverage technology in their client's favor.

It is, of course, always impossible to police quality, even in highly established professions. Quality is really a question of acceptance by the client. Patients decide whether a doctor is great, mediocre, or useless, and opinions about one doctor can vary wildly from patient to patient. In architecture, the client must make a judgment in the mysterious realm of design.

It is not enough to know that a software structure will handle the company's information needs. The client's expectations rise much higher than that. Will the system provide strategic advantage in the areas needed? Will it grow with the company? The employees will be "living" in that system—is it a source of ease and pleasure, or does it increase the aggravation factor? Do the look and feel enhance productivity and satisfaction? Will the company be proud to have this system interface with other businesses and the public?

These are the same questions asked of building designs. The analogy is perfect. And as is the case in all forms of architecture, no code of ethics can guarantee talent or taste. But a code does commit the architect to adhere to high standards of behavior and strive to do his or her best for each client.

Where to Begin

The work of designing and building a profession for software architects is just beginning, that much is quite clear. But even before software architecture is elevated to the status of a formal profession, architecture-driven software construction exists. There are, at the heart of this construction, core practices and ideas that software architects can adopt and their clients can insist upon that will make a profound difference and accelerate the elevation of the profession:

- Software architects accept the analogy with building architecture as being profoundly true. Only with the analogy can clients and users understand and validate the design and construction process. Only with the analogy do architects and builders have clear roles. Software architects are *venustas*—not *utilitas* or *firmitas*. They may assist with building, but their role in the construction phase is guardian of the design.

- Software architects are client advocates who create designs that leverage technology to the client's full advantage. They enter the client's universe to understand the domain, needs, and problems to be solved. The design is a collaborative process with the client.

- Software architects possess a wide breadth of knowledge and skill, not a toolbox limited by pet technologies and inexperience.

- Software architects believe in designing it first and then carefully building it. They present an architectural plan that communicates clearly to both the client and the builders.

- Software architects stand by their work and welcome independent architectural reviews.

- Software architects aspire to fulfill the true classical role of architect and strive for a goal rarely mentioned until now in the software industry, and yet so critical to the future—great design.

In these ways, we can venture to call ourselves *architects* and look forward to the most gratifying moment: when everyone stands together—*utilitas, venustas,* and *firmitas*—to see software that was collectively created now standing strong, and filling with happy inhabitants.

Endnotes

1. Dana Cuff, *Architecture: The Story of Practice* (Cambridge, Mass.: The MIT Press, 1995), 5.

Index

Vitruvian Triad, 52, 63
Vitruvius, architectural theory, 27–28

W

Weehawken, New Jersey, 19
Wolfe, Tom, 40

Workstation failures, 18
Wright, Frank Lloyd, 40
Wrongness of design, 31–32